The Plant World

Mark Lambert

Macdonald/Silver Burdett

Editorial Manager Chester Fisher
Senior Editor Lynne Sabel
Editor John Rowlstone
Assistant Editor Bridget Daly
Series Designers QED (Alaistair Campbell and Edward Kinsey)
Designer Mike Blore
Series Consultant Keith Lye
Consultant John Stidworthy
Production Penny Kitchenham
Picture Research Jenny Golden

© Macdonald Educational Ltd. 1978
First published 1978
Reprinted 1979
Macdonald Educational Ltd.
Holywell House
Worship Street
London EC2A 2EN

Published in the
United States by
Silver Burdett Company
Morristown, N.J.
1980 Printing
ISBN 0-382-06404-6

World of Knowledge

This book breaks new ground in the method it uses to present information to the reader. The unique page design combines narrative with an alphabetical reference section and it uses colourful photographs, diagrams and illustrations to provide an instant and detailed understanding of the book's theme. The main body of information is presented in a series of chapters that cover, in depth, the subject of this book. At the bottom of each page is a reference section which gives, in alphabetical order, concise articles which define, or enlarge on, the topics discussed in the chapter. Throughout the book, the use of SMALL CAPITALS in the text directs the reader to further information that is printed in the reference section. The same method is used to cross-reference entries within each reference section. Finally, there is a comprehensive index at the end of the book that will help the reader find information in the text, illustrations and reference sections. The quality of the text, and the originality of its presentation, ensure that this book can be read both for enjoyment and for the most up-to-date information on the subject.

Contents

Plants Great and Small — 3
No life would be possible on Earth without plants. From the study of fossils, we know that single-celled algae and bacteria were among the first living things on Earth.

How Plants Work — 8
To understand the intricate mechanisms of all living things, including plants, we must study the minute cells of which they are composed. Each cell works like a microscopic factory, making its own special contribution to the miracle of life.

Bacteria and Algae — 17
We often associate bacteria with disease, but they also perform the vital role of breaking down all dead organisms. Bacteria and many algae are microscopic, single-celled plants.

Fungi and Lichens — 21
The familiar mushroom and the tiny pin mould on stale bread belong to the same large division within the plant kingdom – the fungi. Sometimes a fungus lives in a strange plant partnership (called a lichen) with algae.

Mosses and Liverworts — 26
Mosses and liverworts are two related groups of mostly small, simple plants. They are great colonizers because their tiny spores can be carried long distances to new land areas.

Ferns — 30
Ferns, which may be as small as mosses or as large as trees, were common during the Carboniferous period of the Earth's history. Their remains form a large part of the coal seams which were formed at that time.

Gymnosperms — 33
The term gymnosperm comes from two Greek words, meaning 'naked seed'. The most familiar gymnosperms are the conifers, whose seeds are contained in cones. Conifers include some of the world's largest and longest-living trees.

Flowering Plants — 36
Flowering plants, which dominate our countryside and gardens, form the most varied of all plant groups. Botanists call them angiosperms, the Greek for 'enclosed seeds'. They form about 75 per cent of all land-dwelling plants.

Adaptation to Environment — 49
Plants have adapted to cope with all kinds of climate: hot and cold, dry and swampy, salt water and fresh water. Each plant is suited to its own environment and this accounts for the enormous variety of plant life on the Earth.

Plants and Man — 57
All animals, including man, depend on plants for survival. The systematic, scientific cultivation of plants for food has allowed many species to thrive. However, man's progress threatens extinction for many species.

Index — 65

Introduction

The Plant World is a detailed account of the plant kingdom, ranging from single-celled algae to the giant redwoods of California, one of which is more than 111 metres high. It includes a description of how plants have evolved throughout Earth history and there is an important section on plant biology, including descriptions of their cellular structure and how plants make their food, grow and reproduce. Like animals, plants have adapted to a wide variety of environments and **The Plant World** tells of the extraordinary adaptations which have enabled plants to colonize most parts of the globe. Without plants, our Earth would be lifeless. They provide us with food and drink and many other items, ranging from timber and pulp for paper to chemicals used to make medicines, poisons and drugs. Yet many plant species are in danger of extinction, because of the activities of man.

No life would be possible on Earth without plants. From the study of fossils, we know that single-celled algae and bacteria were among the first living things on Earth. Plants have since adapted successfully to almost every known habitat.

Plants Great and Small

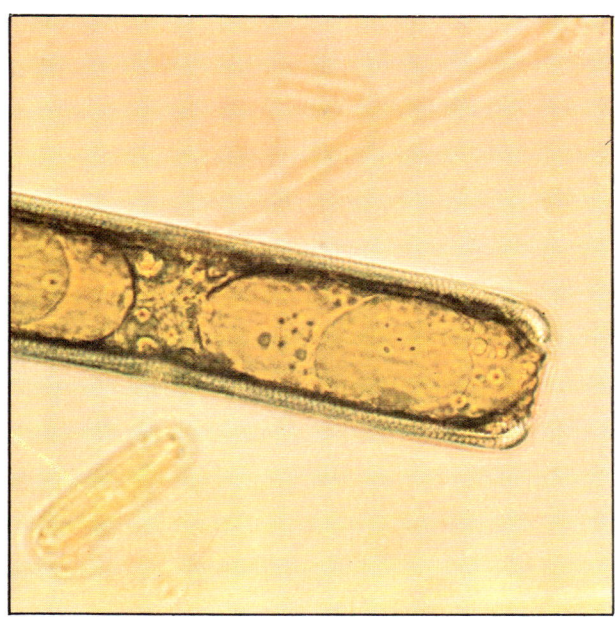

Left: A photomicrograph of the diatom *Pinnularia*. Diatoms belong to the group called algae and are the smallest of all plants.
Below: If a finger nail was enlarged 10 times, a diatom on the same scale would still only be a dot 0.25 mm in diameter.

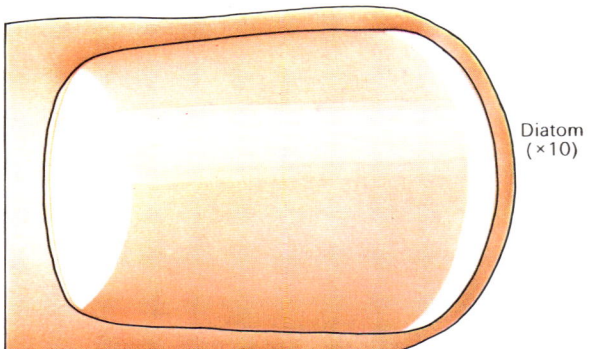

Below right: A Californian coast redwood (*Sequoia sempervivens*) is one of the tallest plants in the world. It may grow to a height of 60-85 metres, and the largest specimen is over 111 metres tall. The redwood is a conifer that may live to be 1,800 years old.

Diatom (×10)

Plants grow in nearly all parts of the world and are found in an incredible variety of shapes and sizes. There are over 360,000 known species of plants in the world. They range from single-celled algae that can only be seen under a microscope to giant redwood trees over 100 metres tall. Some plants live for only a day, others for thousands of years. Other plants are so rare that they only grow in one small area of the world, and even there they prove hard to find. Many plants on the other hand are very common, particularly the grasses that cover a large part of the land.

What are plants?

Many plant varieties are grown for their beauty or for food. However, in addition to man's needs, plants are essential for all life on Earth. Only plants, with the help of sunlight, can build up living material from water, minerals and air.

Like animals, plants have the particular characteristics of living organisms. These are feeding, RESPIRATION, EXCRETION, growth, movement, sensitivity, and REPRODUCTION. However, plants differ from animals in the way in which they perform some of these functions. Animals obtain their food by eating plants or other animals. Plants on the other hand, make their own food by PHOTOSYNTHESIS. Most animals can move from one place to another, and many have muscles that they use for movement. The nervous systems of animals are also used for movement, and for sensing changes in the environment. Plants do not have muscles or nervous systems, and most plants remain in one place. But certain movements, such as phototropism (*see page 47*) do occur.

Of course, there are exceptions to these rules. Fungi could be called the renegades of the plant world as they cannot make their own food by photosynthesis. Some small algae have whip-like organs that enable them to swim.

Reference

A Algae are the simplest groups of plants, belonging to the division Thallophyta. Algae range from single-celled plants to giant seaweeds.
Angiosperms, or flowering plants, are the most advanced group belonging to the division Spermatophyta, subdivision Angiospermae (*see pages 36-48*).

B Bennettitales are an extinct order of gymnosperms (seed-bearing plants) that existed from the Triassic to the Cretaceous periods.
Biomes are major ecological regions of plant and animal life. The plants of a biome make up a FORMATION.
Botany is the study of plants.
Bryophytes are plants belonging to the division Bryophyta. They are divided into 2 classes – the liverworts (Hepaticae) and mosses (Musci) (*see pages 26-29*).

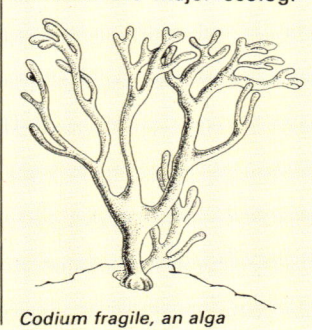

Codium fragile, an alga

C Cambrian period (570-530 million years ago). The period gets its name from *Cambria*, the Latin name for Wales.
Carboniferous period (345-280 million years ago). The period was noted for its vast swampy forests and the appearance of the first seed plants.
Class is one of the groupings used in the classification of plants and animals. A class is divided into ORDERS. In the plant kingdom several classes form a SUBDIVISION.
Classification is the way in which plants and animals are divided into groups and sub-groups. The largest group is a KINGDOM, and the smallest group is a SPECIES.
Climax, see SUCCESSION.
Conifers are a group of

Bennettites

cone-producing, woody plants, belonging to the gymnosperms. They make up the order Coniferales.
Cordaitales are an extinct order of gymnosperms that

Plants Great and Small

Above: The Patriarch Tree in the Sierra Nevada, USA, is the world's largest bristlecone pine (*Pinus aristata*). Some bristlecone pines are the world's oldest known trees. The oldest recorded was 4,900 years old. It grew on the north-east face of Wheeler Peak in California, USA. The oldest-known living tree is the bristlecone pine named Methuselah, which is 4,600 years old and grows in the Californian White Mountains.

The evolution of plants

The Earth was formed about 4,800 million years ago. As it cooled, the first tiny organisms probably formed in the warm seas. The earliest life forms for which we have evidence are blue-green algae. These plants produced lime secretions that later hardened. As a result we now find fossils called stromatolites which consist of many layers of lime laid down by these blue-green algae. Stromatolites dating from 3,100 million years ago have been found in Rhodesia.

The next advance in plant evolution took place in the SILURIAN period. During this time a group of plants called PSILOPHYTES existed. These were marsh plants that probably grew around the edges of lakes. Very few fossils of these plants have been found, but we know that they had tall, branching stems without leaves. At the end of each branch there were one or more capsules that contained spores. Psilophytes were probably the ancestors of the two modern psilotes (primitive plants), *Psilotum* and *Tmesipteris*. No intermediate fossils have been found, and the psilophytes appear to have died out by the end of the Devonian period.

Before the Devonian period we know very little about how plants evolved. But during the Devonian, Carboniferous and Permian periods there existed vast humid forests of plants. This mass of vegetation eventually died and formed peat which compressed into the present-day coal seams. There were several groups in existence at that time: FERNS, horsetails, LYCOPHYTES, PTERIDOSPERMS and CORDAITALES.

The earliest ferns had thick stems and small leaves, but later ferns were very similar to those of today. The lycophytes were the ancestors of modern clubmosses and quillworts. Those that existed during the Carboniferous period, such as *Lepidodendron* and *Calamites*, were tree-sized plants. They produced their spores in the cones like modern members of this group which have

---

existed from the Devonian to the Permian periods.
Cretaceous period (135-65 million years ago). *Creta* is the Latin for chalk.
Cycads are a group of gymnosperms, belonging to the order Cycadales. They were more widespread during the Jurassic and Cretaceous periods, but 9 genera still exist today.

D **de Candolle,** Augustin (1778-1841) was a Swiss botanist who was the first to classify plants by their similarities and differences.
Devonian period (410-345

Cordiates

million years ago). Primitive ferns and lycophytes were evolving at this time.
Division is one of the groupings used in the classification of plants. A division is a sub-group of a KINGDOM, and is divided into several SUBDIVISIONS.

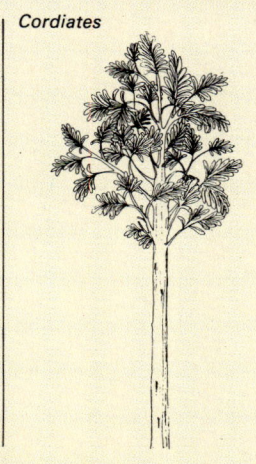

E **Ecology** is the study of plants and animals in relation to their surroundings and to each other.
Environment. This term includes all the conditions in which a plant or animal lives, such as temperature, light, water, and other plants and animals.
Excretion is the process by which a plant or animal gets rid of its waste products.

Stone pine (a conifer)

F **Family** is one of the groupings used in the classification of plants and animals. Several families make up an ORDER, and a family is divided into genera (see GENUS).
Ferns are a group of spore-producing plants related to the LYCOPHYTES. They belong to the division Pteridophyta, subdivision Filicophyta.
Formations are the main natural types of vegetation of the world. They are communities of plants extending over large areas. The type of plant life within a formation is determined by the climate.

Plants Great and Small 5

Pre-Cambrian	Cambrian	Ordovician	Silurian	Devonian	Carboniferous	Permian	Triassic	Jurassic	Cretaceous	Tertiary	Quaternary
600		500		400		300		200		100	0

- **Blue-green algae** — Rivularia
- **Fungi** — Mushroom
- **Algae** — Seaweed
- **Mosses and liverworts** — Moss, Liverwort
- **Psilophytes** — Zosterophyllum, Psilotes, Psilotum
- **Clubmosses and horsetails** — Barawagnathia, Lepidodendron, Calamites, Nathorstiana, Clubmoss, Horsetail
- **Ferns** — Cladoxylon, Etapteris, Fern
- **Cordaitales** — Cordaites, **Conifers** — Conifer
- **Bennettitales** — Williamsonia
- **Ginkgos** — Gingko
- **Pteridosperms** — Diplopteridium, Odontopteris, **Cycads** — Palaeocycas, Cycas
- **Gnetales** — Welwitschia
- **Flowering plants** — Plane tree, Flower

Right: The evolution of the plants we know today has taken place over a period of more than 600 million years. The first plants were single-celled algae, and these probably gave rise directly to the fungi and the algae. The origin of the higher groups is uncertain because we have no fossil evidence that link them with the distant past. It is possible that they all evolved from a common ancestor in the Cambrian or Ordovician periods.

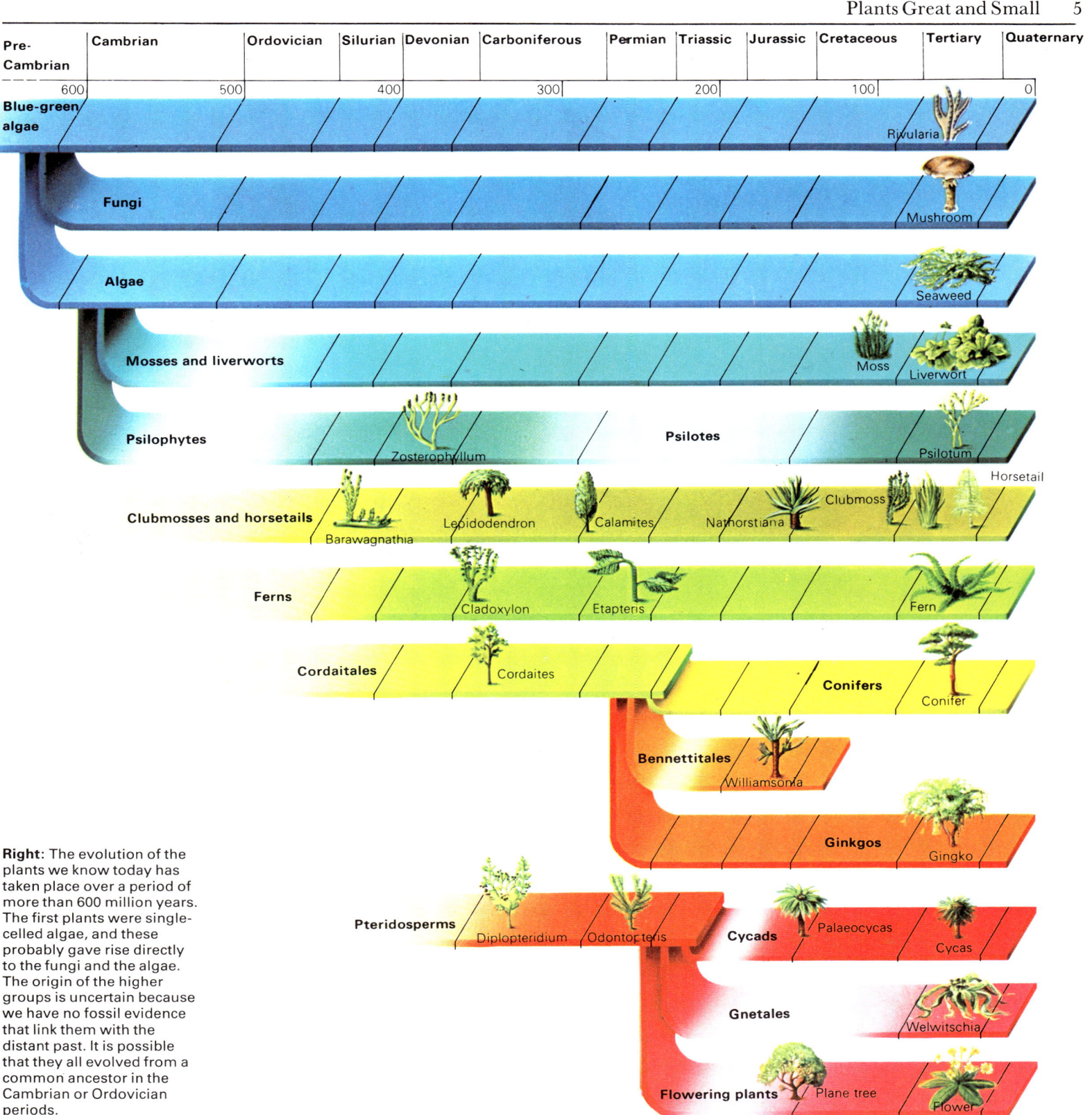

Fungi are a group of plants that do not contain chlorophyll and therefore cannot make their own food. They belong to the division Thallophyta, of which they are a subdivision.

Genus (plural: genera). One of the groupings used in the classification of animals and plants. Several genera make up a FAMILY and a genus is divided into SPECIES.

Ginkgos are a group of gymnosperms. They flourished in the Cretaceous and Tertiary periods. One species, *Ginkgo biloba* (Maidenhair tree), still exists today. Ginkgos belong to the order Ginkgoales.

Gnetales are an order of gymnosperms that consists of only 3 genera (*Gnetum*, *Ephedra* and *Welwitschia*).

Gymnosperms are seed-bearing plants belonging to the division Spermatophyta, subdivision Gymnospermae (see pages 33-35).

Habitat is the local surroundings in which a plant or animal lives. A habitat generally has a particular kind of ENVIRONMENT.

Yew (a conifer)

Hooke, Robert (1635-1703) was an English physicist. He was the first to use the term 'cell', which he discovered by examining the microscopic structure of cork tissue.

Hooker, Joseph (1817-1911) was an English naturalist and the founder of the science of plant geography.

Jurassic period (195-135 million years ago). The name comes from the Jura mountains in France.

Kingdom is the largest grouping used in the classification of living organisms. There are 2 main kingdoms – plants and animals. Some scientists classify all the simple organisms into a third kingdom – Protista. This includes the bacteria, fungi, protozoa, and the unicellular algae.

Linnaeus, Carolus (1707-78) was a Swedish botanist. At an early age he became interested in how the structure of plants differed from one to another. He introduced a new system of classification in his book *Systema Naturae,* which was published in 1735. In particular he introduced the binomial method of naming plants and animals with both generic and specific names.

cones at the top of the shoots.

At the same time as these spore-producing plants existed, the Cordaitales and pteridosperms had developed the ability to produce seeds. Seeds are a more efficient method of reproduction than spores because each plant starts life as a many-celled embryo that is well protected inside the seed case. As a result, seeds survive more easily than spores.

The Cordaitales were tall trees that formed large forests in the Carboniferous period. But by the end of the Permian period they were extinct. The conifers, Ginkgos and BENNETTITALES evolved from the Cordaitales. The Ginkgos flourished during the Cretaceous period, but today the only survivor of this group is the Maidenhair tree, *Ginkgo biloba*. The Bennettitales looked like CYCADS and bore seeds in structures that resembled flowers. But despite this, they were probably not related to either cycads or flowering plants.

The pteridosperms, or 'seed ferns', resembled true FERNS in many ways except that they produced seeds at the ends of special branches. This group flourished during the Carboniferous period, but became extinct during the Triassic period. The cycads, Gnetales, and the flowering plants evolved from the pteridosperms.

Above: The monkey puzzle tree (*Auracaria araucana*) is one of the few trees that live at high altitudes. It is also one of the few conifers found in the Southern Hemisphere, living in the Andes Mountains of South America.

Cycads are palm-like plants. Many types existed during the Cretaceous period, but only nine genera exist today. The Gnetales are an odd group of only three genera — *Welwitschia*, *Ephedra*, and *Gnetum*. They are classed as gymnosperms but show many characteristics of flowering plants.

The most important group, however, is the flowering plants, or angiosperms. During the Cretaceous and Tertiary periods they increased rapidly in number, and today they are the dominant group of plants. There are two main reasons for their success. First, they have been able to adapt to almost every habitat in the world. Secondly, they have extremely efficient methods of producing and dispersing seeds (*see page 40*).

Where plants live

The type of vegetation that can be found in a particular area is determined by the ENVIRONMENT. Both the climate and the geography of the region affect the nature of the plants that are found. The natural world can be divided into several BIOMES, each of which contains a distinct plant FORMATION. The richest of all the biomes is the tropical rain forest. Vegetation of this type occurs in areas near the equator that have a high

Below and right: The alpine areas of the world contain many unique plant forms. In the highest regions only lichens and mosses can survive the cold. But well below the snow-line coniferous forest is mixed with rich pasture.

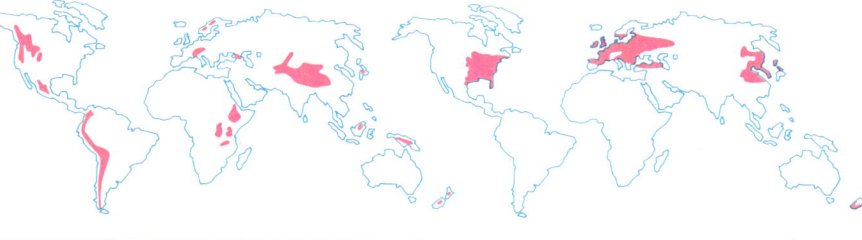

Below and left: The deciduous forests of the world contain broad-leaved trees such as the beech and silver birch. Many other plants, including ferns and mosses can be found growing in the leaf litter among the trees.

Lycophytes are a group of plants belonging to the division Pteridophyta, subdivision Lycophyta. They include the clubmosses, quillworts and horsetails (see pages 26-29).

Mendel, Gregor (1822-84) was an Austrian botanist who was also an Augustinian monk. His great interest in plants led him to perform breeding experiments on pea plants. His discovery of certain 'factors' that could be passed from one generation to the next laid the foundations for the science of genetics, understood only after his death.
Morphology is the study of shape and form.

Carolus Linnaeus

Order is one of the groupings used in the classification of plants and animals. An order is divided into FAMILIES, and several orders make up a CLASS.

Palaeobotany is the study of fossil plants.
Permian period (280-230 million years ago). The name comes from the Perm district of the Ural mountains in Russia.
Photosynthesis is the process by which plants make food, in the form of sugar, from water and carbon dioxide in the presence of sunlight and chlorophyll (see page 13).
Plant ecology, see ECOLOGY.
Pre-Cambrian refers to the period of time before the beginning of the CAMBRIAN PERIOD.
Psilophytes are an extinct group of plants that existed during the Devonian period. They belong to the division Pteridophyta, subdivision Psilophyta, class Psilophytopsida, order Psilophytales. They are possibly the ancestors of the modern psilotes (a small group of modern plants with primitive features). Some of their fossils have been found in Scotland.
Psilotes, see PSILOPHYTES.
Pteridophytes are a group

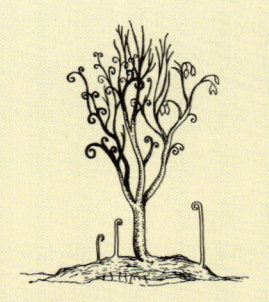

Psilophyton

Plants Great and Small 7

rainfall. A tropical climate is suitable for continuous plant growth, and its rain forests contain large trees, usually evergreen, together with other exotic species of plants.

In climates where growth cannot be continuous because of seasonal variations in temperature, the type of vegetation changes dramatically. In temperate regions two main biomes occur — grassland and temperate forest. In grassland regions, herb vegetation dominates, together with some shrubs and trees. Temperate forests may be deciduous or coniferous. The former shed their leaves in autumn whilst the latter are evergreen. The exact nature of the plant life depends very much on the seasonal variations of climate. For example, if there is any winter frost, many plant species cannot survive. Many non-woody plants have adapted to these conditions by remaining dormant during the winter months.

The harshest biomes are those where it is either very cold or very hot. In such areas the density of plant life is very much reduced. Montane biomes include the tundra and mountain regions, where it is so cold that only the hardiest plants can survive. This is also true of desert conditions, and there are many other environments where only specially adapted plants can live (*see pages 49-56*).

Above: Life began in the oceans of the world and they still contain a wide variety of plant life, such as *Laminaria*, a brown seaweed. *Laminaria* belongs to the algae group which includes most of the sea plants.

The study of plant formations and world vegetation zones is included in the science of plant geography. This subject also deals with the spread of plant groups and species. For example, we know that cacti originated in South America, but birds and man have carried their seeds far afield. They are still gradually spreading into all the areas to which they are suited.

Plant geography also includes the study of the effects of natural barriers, such as mountains and oceans. For example, *Pinus sylvestris*, the Scots pine, is one of the dominant trees in northern Europe. However, it is not found in the natural vegetation of North America. The Atlantic and Pacific Oceans have prevented this species from spreading.

PLANT ECOLOGY is concerned with the more detailed study of the vegetation of an area or locality. For example, the ecology of an area of deciduous woodland or chalk grassland can be studied to learn which species of plants are present. All the plants living in such habitats are suited to the local conditions of climate and soil. At the same time, they are suited to living together within a plant community. Plants are influenced to a great extent by others around them, particularly when there is competition for sunlight, space and soil nutrients.

Below and right: The tropical regions of the world include many areas of rain forest. In this forest lianas – the long stems of woody climbing plants – can be seen together with a climbing palm tree.

Below and left: The map of the world shows that the tundra includes part of Alaska. Few plants can grow in the Arctic regions of the northern tundra, but Alaska can support some hardy flowers in summer.

---

of spore-producing plants, belonging to the division Pteridophyta. This includes all the ferns, lycophytes, psilophytes and psilotes.
Pteridosperms are a group of extinct gymnosperms that existed from the Devonian to the Triassic periods. They belong to the order Pteridospermales.

Q Quaternary period (2 million years ago to the present day). The name comes from the fact that geologists formerly divided fossil-bearing rocks into 4 periods.

R Reproduction is the process in which an organism produces a new individual.
Respiration is the process in which an organism takes in oxygen and uses it to 'burn' food to provide itself with energy. During the process carbon dioxide is formed and released (*see pages 8-16*).

S Silurian period (440-410 million years ago). The name comes from the *Silures*, an ancient tribe who lived in the area of Wales where rocks of this period

were first studied. The first land plants were probably evolving at this time.
Species is the smallest group used in the classifica-

Pteridosperm

tion of plants and animals. Members of the same species can successfully breed with each other but they cannot breed with members of another species.
Subdivision is one of the groupings used in the classification of plants. A subdivision is divided into CLASSES, and several subdivisions make up a DIVISION.
Succession is the gradual, progressive change from simple, hardy plants, such as lichens and mosses, towards more advanced plants during the colonization of a

piece of land. When the succession is complete, and the plant community is stable, a climax has been reached.

T Taxonomy is the detailed study of the classification of plants and animals.
Tertiary period (65-2 million years ago). The name is derived in the same way as the QUATERNARY PERIOD.
Triassic period (225-195 million years ago) is so named because of a 3 layered area of rock in Germany that dates from this time.

To understand the intricate mechanisms of all living things, including plants, we must study the minute cells of which they are composed. Each cell works like a microscopic factory, making its own special contribution to the miracle of life.

How Plants Work

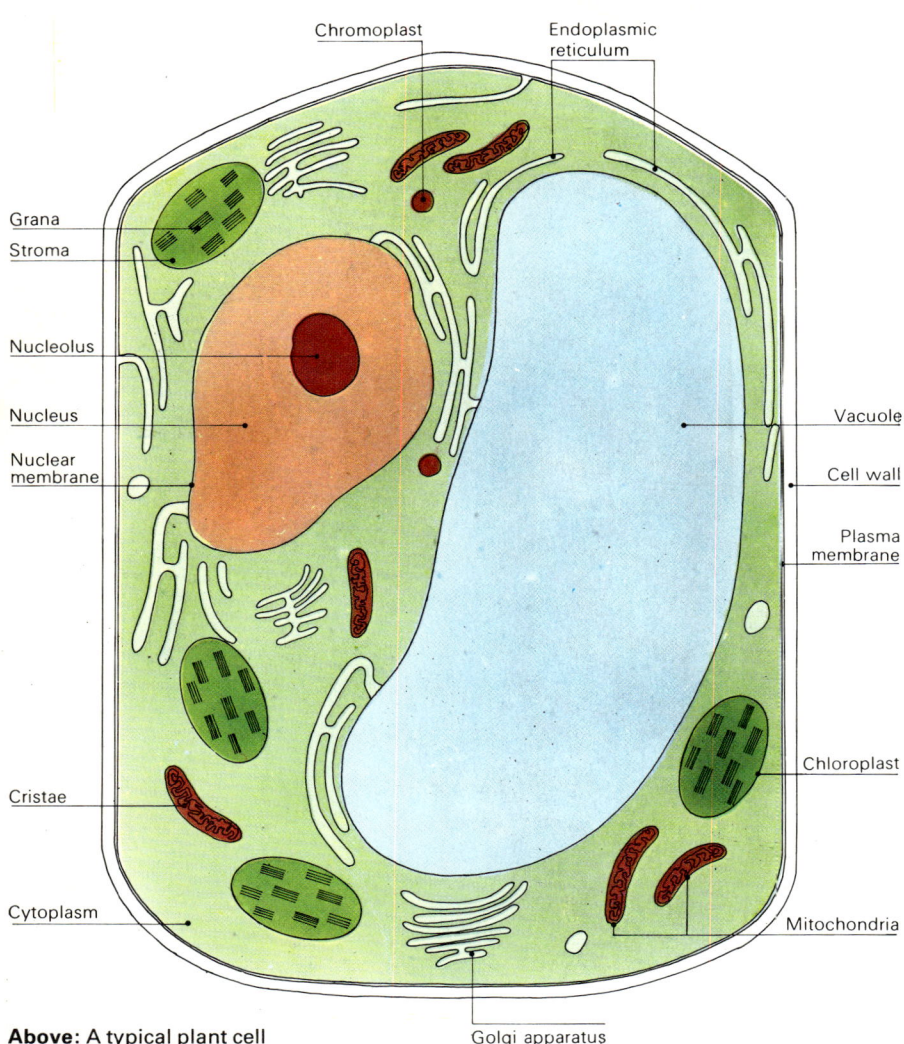

Above: A typical plant cell consists of a cellulose cell wall that encloses the cytoplasm and the nucleus. In the cytoplasm there are several structures that do the work of the cell. The nucleus controls and co-ordinates this work. The vacuole is a space inside the cell filled with a watery fluid.

Plants and animals are made up entirely of CELLS. A plant cell is like a tiny enclosed box. It contains all the chemicals and structures that the plant needs in order to live. Neighbouring cells work together so that the functions of the whole plant are co-ordinated. But at the same time, each cell works by itself like a tiny factory.

The outer covering of a cell is called the cell wall. Each cell is connected to its neighbour by tiny holes in these cell walls. Chemicals can pass through these holes from one cell to the next. The contents of each cell consist of the NUCLEUS and the CYTOPLASM.

The nucleus is the central controller of the cell – like a computer centre in a factory. It contains thread-like structures called CHROMOSOMES. These contain all the information needed to organize the activities of the rest of the cell. The information is contained in a chemical compound called DNA, and the information is carried to where it is needed by RNA.

The cytoplasm consists of a watery mixture that includes a number of important solid structures called ORGANELLES. These are the working parts of the factory. Some organelles use the chemicals imported into the cell to make other chemicals that are useful to the plant, such as SUGARS and PROTEINS. Other organelles help to produce energy for the plant.

Proteins are a very important group of chemical products. They are made on a thin folded membrane in the cytoplasm, called the ENDOPLASMIC RETICULUM. The proteins that a cell makes may be used for growth or for repairing damage. On the other hand, they may be special proteins called ENZYMES. These are essential for the plant. Without them, many of the chemical reactions that take place in cells could not occur.

All the activities of a cell require energy. This is provided by the MITOCHONDRIA, which are the

Reference

A **Amino acids** are the chemicals that form the 'building blocks' of PROTEINS. When a protein is formed, amino acids become joined together into long chains. There are 21 different amino acids that go to make up proteins. Different combinations of amino acids make different proteins. The general formula for amino acids is $R.CH(NH_2).COOH$, where R can be any group of atoms (usually carbon and hydrogen atoms). The simplest amino acid is glycine.
Anabolism is the building up of complicated molecules from simpler ones, using energy. An example is the building up of sugar and starch molecules during photosynthesis. See also CATABOLISM, METABOLISM.

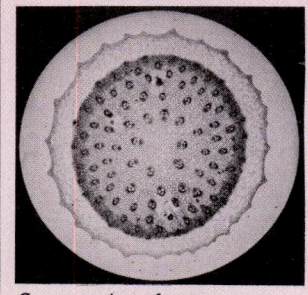

Cross-section of a stem

C **Carbohydrates** are chemical compounds composed of carbon, hydrogen and oxygen. They include sugars, starch and cellulose, all of which are important in plants.
Catabolism is the breaking down of complicated molecules into simple molecules, releasing energy at the same time. An example is the breakdown of sugar into water and carbon dioxide during respiration. See also ANABOLISM, METABOLISM.
Cells are the basic units of life. A plant cell consists of a small quantity of protoplasm surrounded by a plasma membrane and a cellulose cell wall.
Cellulose is a CARBOHYDRATE substance that is the basic constituent of the cell walls of plants. It is made up of long chains of glucose molecules. Glucose is one of the sugars made during photosynthesis.
Cell wall (the outer layer of a plant cell). In young cells the wall is a thin primary wall made of cellulose, together with a few other chemicals. The primary wall is crossed by PLASMODESMATA.

Chrysanthemums

'power-houses' of the cell — like electrical generators in a factory. Respiration is the energy-producing process and it takes place inside the mitochondria.

Like full-scale factories, cells have to get rid of their waste products and export some of the materials they make. The main waste product is the carbon dioxide produced during respiration. This diffuses through the cell wall. The remaining waste products either diffuse out, or they are stored in the cell in a solid, insoluble form. Many chemicals exported by the cell also diffuse out, but molecules of some elements are too large to pass through the cell membrane. They are probably removed from the cell by a structure called the GOLGI APPARATUS.

Cells for different purposes

The simplest cells of all are found in the regions where growth is taking place. They are small, cube-shaped cells with thin cell walls, and completely filled with cytoplasm. As the region of growth moves away, they begin to grow. However, the amount of cytoplasm increases very little. Thus, as a cell grows larger, its cytoplasm stretches and a space, or VACUOLE, is formed.

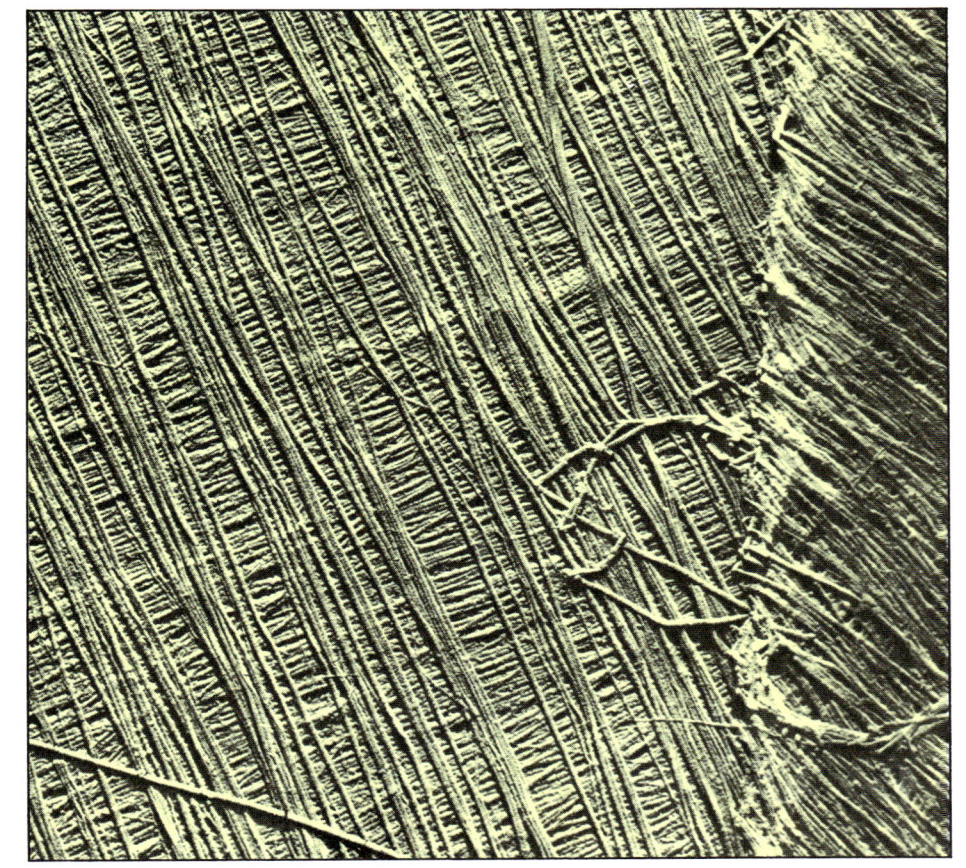

Left: This photograph was taken through an electron microscope. It is a portion of a plant cell wall – magnified 30,000 times. The cellulose fibres of the wall can be seen clearly.

Above: Cork comes from the bark of the cork oak (*Quercus suber*). Robert Hooke (1635-1703) discovered that cork is made up of millions of tiny compartments, which he called cells.

The eventual function of a cell depends on its position in the plant. Therefore, as cells grow they become differentiated — that is, cells with different functions differ in shape and structure.

A large proportion of cells become PARENCHYMA CELLS. These make up a great deal of the plant body, especially in young plants. They have thin cells walls made up of a substance called CELLULOSE. They often contain storage products, such as starch grains. COLLENCHYMA CELLS are firmer cells. They have cell walls that are thickened with cellulose, often in the corners of the cells. The stems of the larger non-woody plants need the firm support given by collenchyma cells. Where even more support is needed, non-living stiffening cells are found, such as SCLERENCHYMA FIBRES and STONE CELLS. These

---

In older, thickened cells, a secondary wall is laid down inside the primary wall. This may be made of cellulose, or lignin and cellulose, or lignin and cutin. It is generally perforated by pits, which allow connections between cells. Between the cell walls of adjacent cells lies the MIDDLE LAMELLA.

Chloroplasts are small chlorophyll-containing bodies in the cytoplasm of a cell. This is the site of photosynthesis. A chloroplast consists of a double membrane surrounding a material called the stroma. Embedded in the stroma are grana, and it is here that photosynthesis takes place. The grana are composed of a number of round disks, which are stacked like coins. The disks carry the chlorophyll.

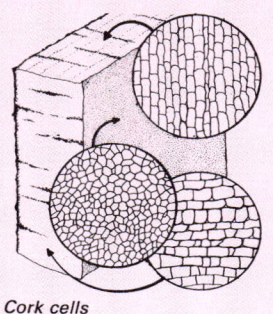

Chlorosis is a disease of plants in which the leaves turn yellow. This is because the plant cannot make chlorophyll, either through lack of light or lack of certain minerals, such as magnesium.

Chromatin is the granular material in the nucleus of a cell. It consists of PROTEIN, DNA, and RNA.

Chromoplasts are small bodies in the cytoplasm that contain pigments. Those that contain chlorophyll are called CHLOROPLASTS. Other chromoplasts may contain carotenes, xanthophylls, anthocyanins or other pigments.

Cork cells

May blossom

Chromosomes are thread-like bodies in the nucleus of a cell. They consist mostly of DNA and protein. A normal cell has several pairs of chromosomes. The 2 members of each pair are identical in appearance. They are called homologous chromosomes. The body cells of a particular species always contain the same number of pairs of chromosomes. The broad bean (*Vicia faba*) has 6 pairs; the onion (*Allium cepa*) has 8 pairs. Man has 23 pairs.

Collenchyma is a cell tissue that helps to provide support

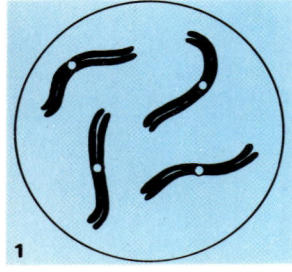

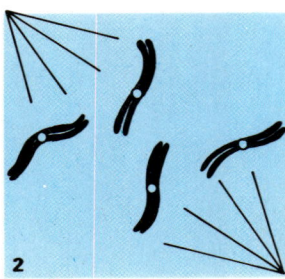

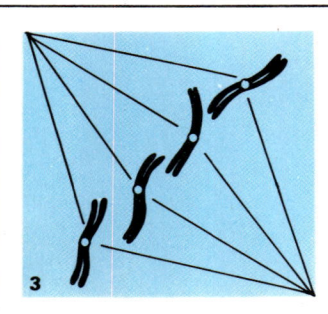

Above: In mitosis 2 new cells are formed. **1.** At the beginning of division the chromosomes are already divided into chromatids. The nuclear membrane is still present. **2.** A fibre-like structure, the spindle, forms. The nuclear membrane disappears. **3.** The chromosomes are arranged on the centre of the spindle. **4.** The chromatids move apart and move towards opposite sides of the cell. **5.** A new cell wall forms down the middle of the cell. Two new nuclear membranes form around the new chromosomes. The number of chromosomes in the 2 new cells is the same as the number in the original cell.

Left: A plant in full turgor is erect and healthy.

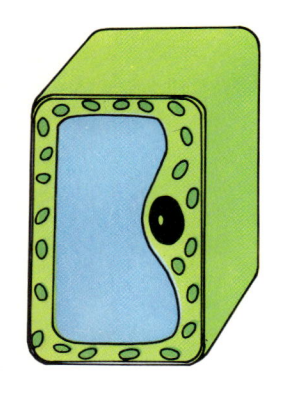

Above: The cells of a plant in full turgor contain the maximum amount of water possible. Hence they are stiff and strong.

cells have walls that are thickened with substances called CUTIN and LIGNIN.

As well as support, a plant needs protection. Leaves and stems of non-woody plants are covered in a layer of cells called the EPIDERMIS. The exact shape of these cells varies from plant to plant, but they are roughly cube-shaped. On the outer surface of the epidermis is a layer of cutin called the cuticle. Some plants have hairs or prickles, which are composed of modified epidermal cells.

As a plant gets older and becomes woody, the epidermis on its stem and branches is replaced by cork cells, which make up the bark. The cell walls of cork cells are lined with a completely waterproof substance called suberin. As a result, the contents of the cells die, and cork becomes a non-living tissue.

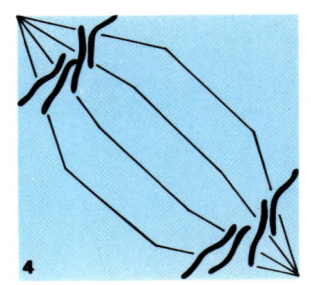

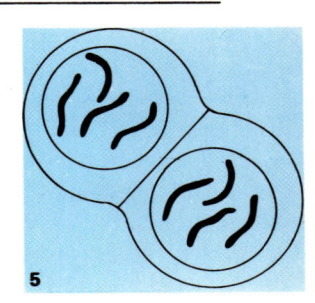

Water and food move from cell to cell relatively slowly, and so plants have developed 'plumbing systems' that can move materials more rapidly through the plant. XYLEM cells conduct water up the plant from the root to the leaves. They are non-living, elongated cells that are joined end-to-end to form a continuous system of pipes. The walls of xylem cells are thick. A secondary wall is present, made up of cellulose and lignin. In some cases it may take the form of rings around the inside of the xylem cell. Even in heavily-thickened xylem cells the secondary wall is perforated by pits.

PHLOEM cells conduct food and other material up and down the plant. Like xylem cells they are elongated, but they are not open at both ends. Instead, the end walls that lead from one phloem cell to another are perforated like sieves. Hence, the dividing wall between phloem cells is called a sieve plate. A phloem cell, or sieve tube, is a living cell. It contains cytoplasm, but it does not have a nucleus. As a result, each phloem cell has to be controlled by one or two companion cells.

Dividing cells

There are two processes by which cells divide — MITOSIS and MEIOSIS. As a plant grows larger, new cells are needed. These are produced by mitosis, which occurs in all the growing parts of a plant. Meiosis produces sex cells and occurs in the reproductive organs of a plant.

The aim of mitosis is to produce two new cells that are identical in every respect to the original cell. Most parts of the cell divide quite simply, but the nucleus has to undergo a more complicated process in order to make sure that the new cells have the same number and type of chromosomes.

During the course of mitosis, each chromosome divides into two chromatids. The chromatids are drawn apart, one to each end of

---

for young growing plants. It is found in the stems, leaves and leaf stalks. The cells are usually thickened in the corners, but they are still capable of growing lengthwise.
Cutin is a waterproof substance made up of a number of complicated long-chain molecules. The basic chemicals that form these long chains are carbon compounds called fatty acids.
Cytoplasm consists of all the contents in a cell except the nucleus.

D **DNA** (Deoxyribonucleic acid) is the chemical compound in the nucleus of a cell that carries the genetic information. It is made up of long strands of linked sugar and phosphate molecules. Attached to the sugar groups are 4 chemical compounds called bases — adenine, thymine, guanine, and cytosine. In a complete molecule of DNA, 2 strands coil round each other in a structure called a double helix that resembles a spiral staircase. The rungs of this 'staircase' are formed by pairs of the bases. Adenine pairs with thymine, and guanine pairs with cytosine.

Silver fir

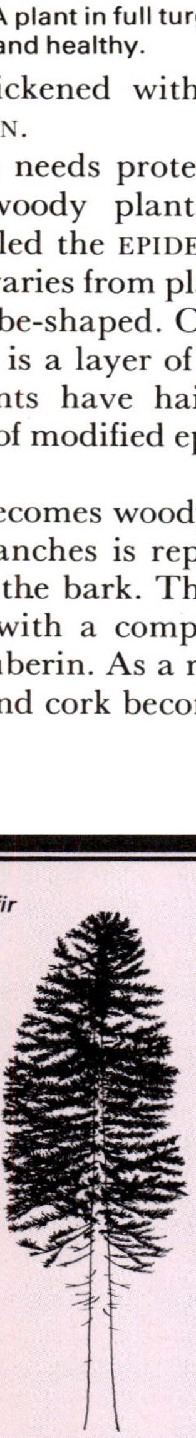

The order in which the bases occur determines the information that is passed from the nucleus by RNA. It also determines the genetic information passed to the next generation.

E **Endoplasmic reticulum.** This is a complicated system of channels present in the CYTOPLASM of a cell. On the surface of its membranes are the RIBOSOMES, and the whole structure is concerned with making PROTEINS.
Enzymes are carbon compounds that act as catalysts for the chemical reactions that occur in living cells. Thus, they help certain reactions to take place, but they do not actually take part. The enzymes are not changed during the process. Sometimes an enzyme needs to become attached to a coenzyme in order to work.
Epidermis. This is the outer layer of cells of a plant stem, leaf or root. The epidermis of a stem or leaf is usually covered with a waterproof cuticle made of CUTIN.

F **Fats and oils** are carbon compounds that are fre-

the cell, where they become new chromosomes. When this is complete, the remainder of the cell divides.

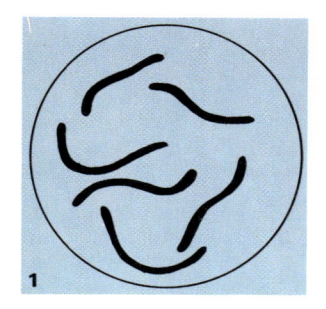

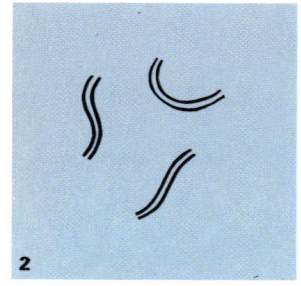

Sex cells, on the other hand, are not identical to their parent cell. During reproduction two sex cells fuse together. However, when this happens the number of chromosomes is not doubled. This is because during meiosis the number of chromosomes is halved. Thus, when the sex cells fuse, the resulting cell contains the normal number of chromosomes. Meiosis is therefore often called 'reduction division'. The halving of the number of chromosomes is achieved by two divisions of the nucleus, in which the chromosomes divide only once.

Plants and water

Water is essential for the survival of a plant. A tree consists of about 50 per cent water, and a non-woody plant consists of about 75 per cent water. A plant must have water in its cells so that all the organelles and enzymes can function properly. Without water, the chemical reactions of respiration and photosynthesis could not occur.

Water is also needed for support, particularly in non-woody plants. It is taken up through the tiny ROOT HAIRS by a process called OSMOSIS. The same process causes water to pass from cell to cell. As a cell fills with water, its walls become stretched. When the cell can hold no more water it is described as having maximum TURGOR PRESSURE. In this condition the cell is stiff, and it is therefore turgor pressure that keeps a non-woody plant erect. When there is not enough water in the cells, the plant wilts.

The root hairs of a plant provide an enormous surface area through which water can be absorbed. The water passes through the cells of the root, and from there it is pushed into the xylem vessels of the root by ROOT PRESSURE. The xylem vessels carry the water up the stem to the leaves. From here a considerable amount of water is lost by evaporation, passing out through the leaf STOMATA. This water loss is called transpiration.

Transpiration has two main uses. Firstly, the evaporation from the leaves has a cooling effect. Plants lose much more water by transpiration on hot days. The rate of transpiration can be controlled by opening and closing the leaf stomata. Secondly, essential minerals are taken up from the soil and carried into the plant by the transpiration stream — the name given to the flow of water from the roots up through the stem and out through the leaves.

At one time botanists could not understand how water moved up a plant. Root pressure alone was not enough to drive water up a tree

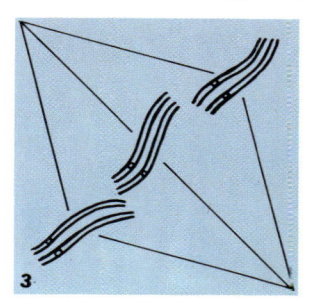

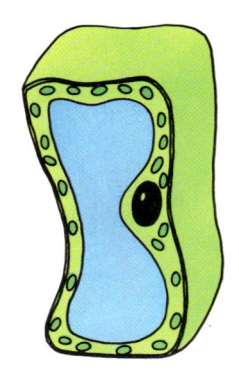

Above: In meiosis 4 new cells are formed. **1.** The chromosomes appear as long, thin threads. They are *not* split, as in mitosis. **2.** The chromosomes shorten and pair off. **3.** Each chromosome divides into 2 chromatids. Then, still in their pairs, they are organized on the spindle. **4.** The chromosomes are drawn apart. **5.** The 2 cells that have been formed by the first division divide again. But this time the chromosomes do not divide. The chromatids formed in the first division are drawn apart – as in mitosis. Thus the number of chromosomes in each of the 4 new cells is half the number in the original cell.

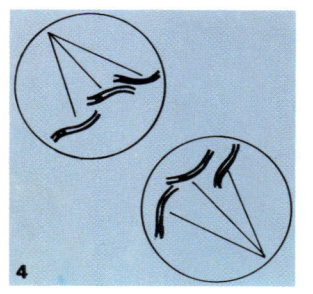

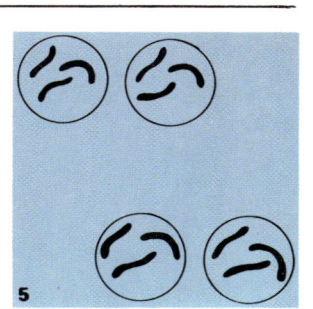

Right: A plant that has insufficient water wilts.

Above: The cells of a wilting plant are weak and bendable. This is because they do not contain enough water to keep the cell wall stiff.

---

quently found as storage products in plants. For example, they are found as food reserves in the seeds of the coconut palm (*Cocos nucifera*) and the cocoa plant (*Theobroma cacao*). They are all derived from compounds called fatty acids.

G Golgi apparatus. This is a small body in the cytoplasm of a cell. It is similar to the ENDOPLASMIC RETICULUM, and consists of membranes folded into sacs, or vesicles. Its function is probably the export of substances out of the cell.

L Lignin is a complicated chemical compound that gives strength to cell walls. It is composed of long chains of carbon compounds.

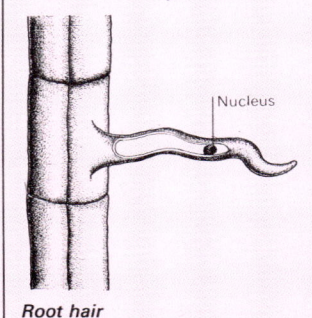

Root hair

M Meiosis is the process of cell division that forms sex cells. During this process the number of chromosomes in the nucleus is halved.

Mesophyll cells are irregular cells that form the spongy tissue in the lower part of the leaf of a flowering plant. There are air spaces between the cells to allow carbon dioxide and oxygen to pass into and out of the cells.

Metabolism includes all the chemical processes of an organism, involving ANABOLISM and CATABOLISM.

Middle lamella. This is the thin layer that cements adjacent cell walls together. It is made of a substance called pectin, together with other similar CARBOHYDRATE compounds.

Mineral salts are chemicals present in the soil, such as potassium nitrate and magnesium sulphate. In the soil they dissolve in water and form ions. In this form they are taken up in the transpiration stream of a plant, supplying it with potassium, magnesium, nitrogen and sulphur.

Mitochondria are micros-

False acacia

copic bodies present in the cytoplasm of a cell. They are the energy-producing ORGANELLES of the cell, and it is here that respiration takes

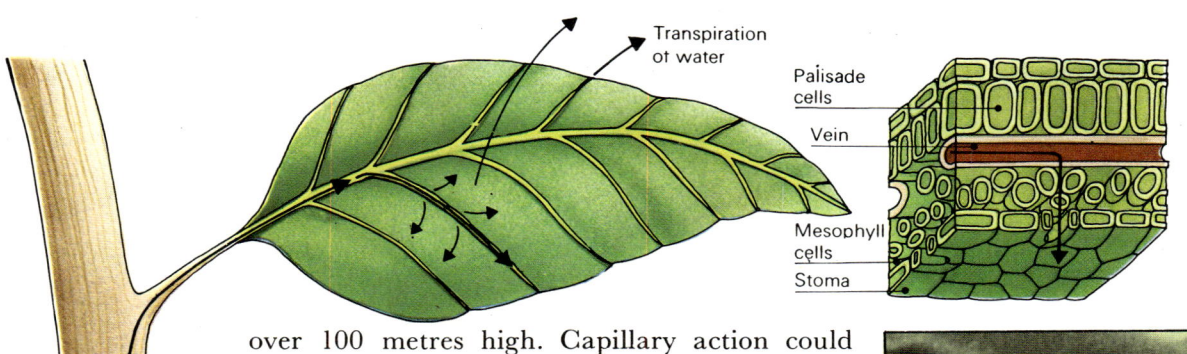

How Plants Work

Left: The transpiration stream ends in the leaf. Water passes along the thin veins of xylem cells. From there it diffuses into the mesophyll layer and out through the stomata on the underside of the leaf.
Below: A photograph of the stomata of a leaf — magnified 5,400 times. Each stoma has 2 guard cells.

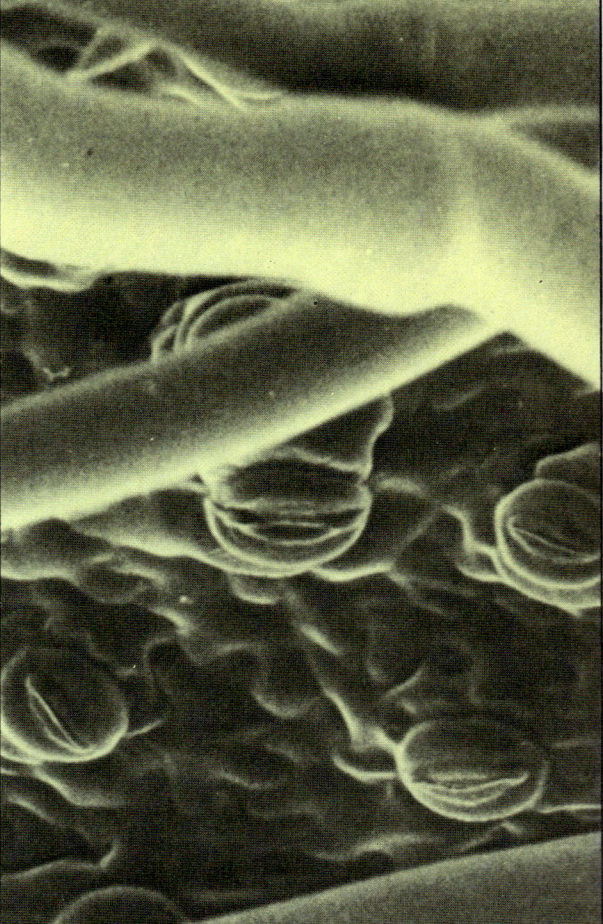

Above and below: Water passes up the stem via the xylem vessels in the vascular bundles.

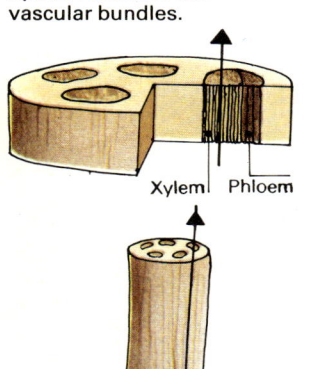

over 100 metres high. Capillary action could draw up water only a few metres. Various theories were put forward, including some that suggested that there was a pumping action by some of the living cells in the stem.

In fact, water is quite simply pulled up the plant by transpiration. This is made possible only by a very special property of water. Its molecules have a strong tendency to cling together. This property is called cohesion. As water molecules leave the xylem vessels in the leaf, others are drawn in to take their place. Due to this cohesion, the leaf of a 100-metre tree can exert a pull of over 100 atmospheres (103 kilogrammes per square centimetre) — enough to draw water up from its roots.

Plants and energy

The living world obtains all its energy from the Sun. The small fraction of the Sun's energy that reaches the Earth arrives in the form of heat and light. The heat keeps the atmosphere and the surface of the Earth warm enough to support life. Some of the light that falls on the Earth's surface is used by plants to start the energy chain that keeps the living world functioning.

The method whereby plants are able to trap and use light energy is called photosynthesis. Plants use light to make food. The food may be used for the plant's own energy needs, or the plants may be eaten by animals. In this way the

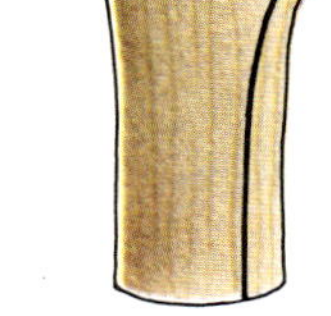

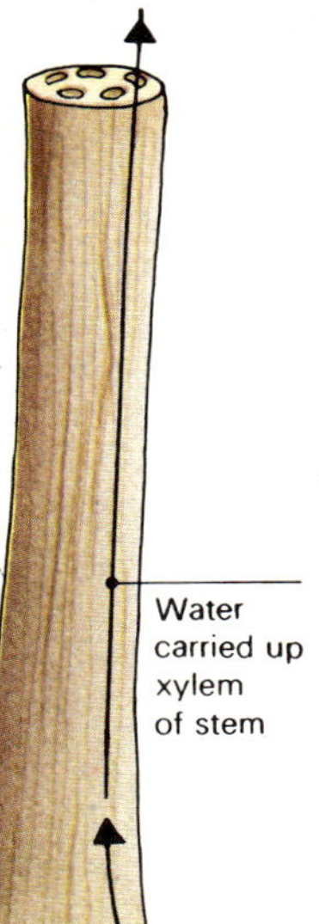

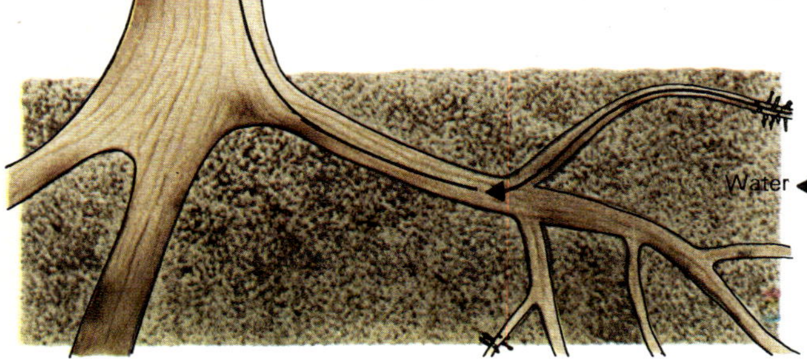

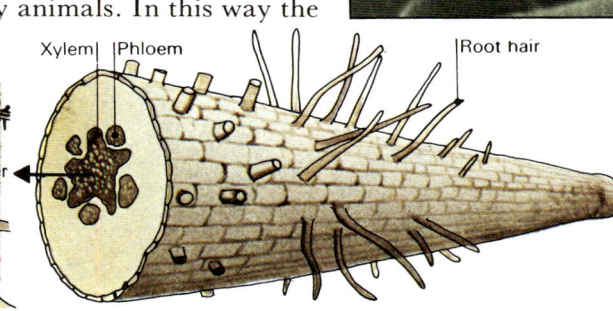

Left: The flow of water through a plant, the transpiration stream, begins in the root. Water is taken into the root via the root hairs. From there it passes through the root tissues into the central core of xylem vessels. The xylem vessels of the root connect with those of the stem.

---

place. Each mitochondrion is surrounded by a double membrane. The inner membrane is folded inwards to form cristae. Respiration occurs on these cristae.
Mitosis is the process of cell division that forms new cells in an organism.

N Nuclear membrane. This membrane surrounds the nucleus of a cell. It is perforated by a number of pores which allow RNA to pass through. The ENDOPLASMIC RETICULUM is connected to the pores in the nuclear membrane.

Nucleolus. This is a small dense body in the nucleus of a cell. Its function is to make RIBOSOMES. A nucleolus consists of larger amounts of RNA and protein, together with a small amount of chromosomal DNA, known as the nucleolar organizer.
Nucleus. This contains the CHROMOSOMES of a cell. It is the central organizer of the cell. When a cell divides, the nucleus divides into 2 new identical nuclei.

O Organelles are structures in the cytoplasm of a cell that have particular specialized functions. The main organelles of a plant cell include the CHLOROPLASTS, MITOCHONDRIA, and the ENDOPLASMIC RETICULUM.

Osmosis

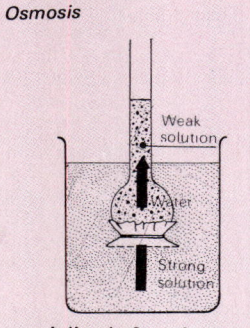

Osmosis is the passage of water through a SEMI-PERMEABLE MEMBRANE from a weaker solution to a stronger one. The pressure needed to prevent this passage of water is called the osmotic pressure, which is greater when the solution is stronger. A weak solution is said to have a high diffusion pressure. Water thus passes from a solution that has a high diffusion pressure to a solution that has a low diffusion pressure. In a laboratory experiment using 2 sugar solutions separated by a semi-permeable membrane, osmosis continues until the solutions are the same strength. The root cells of plants have a lower diffusion pressure than the soil

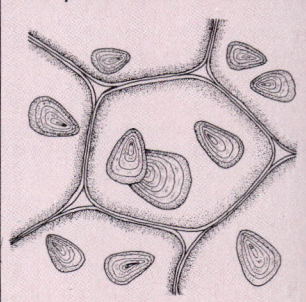

Parenchyma cells

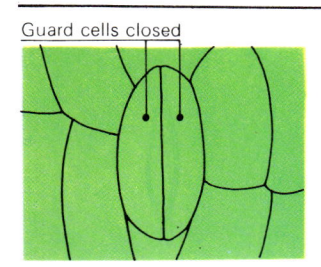

How Plants Work

Left: The stomata of a leaf are the openings from which water escapes from the plant during transpiration. But they are also the 'breathing pores' of the plant. Generally stomata are open during the day (*below*) and are closed at night (*left*). In extreme conditions of drought the stomata may close during the day when the plant wilts.

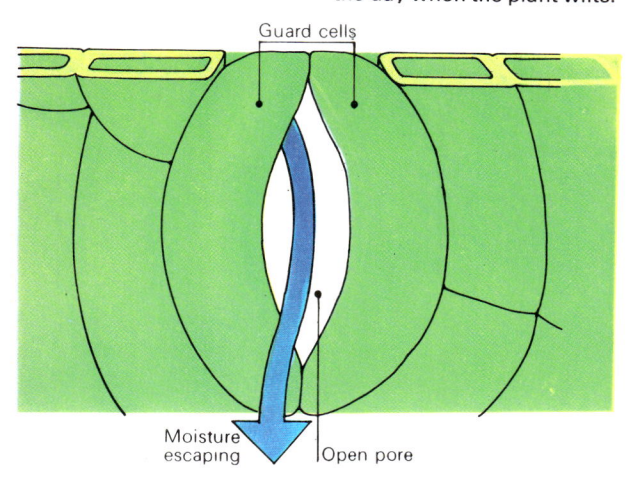

Below: Photosynthesis can only take place in the light. Thus the leaves of a plant are always arranged so that they receive the maximum possible amount of light. Trees, such as these beech trees, have most of their leaves spread out sideways. The leaves are also tilted, presenting the greatest surface area to the sunlight.

energy contained in the food is passed on. Animals use the energy in movement and other activities of the body. Eventually, both animals and plants die, and bacteria use the energy as they play their part in the decay of living matter. In whatever way the energy is used it is ultimately converted to heat. This radiates out into the atmosphere, and from there is lost into space.

Thus, the secret of life on Earth is the chemical that enables photosynthesis to take place. This chemical is chlorophyll. It is a green pigment made up of complicated molecules. One essential ingredient of the chlorophyll molecule is magnesium, which must therefore be one of the minerals taken up from the soil in the transpiration stream. Chlorophyll is contained in the CHLOROPLASTS, and it is here that photosynthesis takes place.

Photosynthesis, like many of the chemical processes of life, is a long chain of chemical reactions. However, it is basically the conversion of carbon dioxide and water into sugar. The carbon dioxide is taken from the air, and oxygen is released. Some of this sugar is converted to starch by the action of ENZYMES.

---

water around them. Thus, water passes into the cells from the soil. Inside the plant, osmosis causes water to pass from one cell to another. But a cell cannot take in water indefinitely. The cell wall exerts TURGOR PRESSURE. This limits the amount of water taken in, and the internal solution does not necessarily become equal in strength to the external solution. *See also* SUCTION PRESSURE.

P Palisade cells form the tissue in the upper part of the leaf of a flowering plant. They are elongated cells that contain large numbers of CHLOROPLASTS. Most of the photosynthesis that occurs in the plant takes place here.

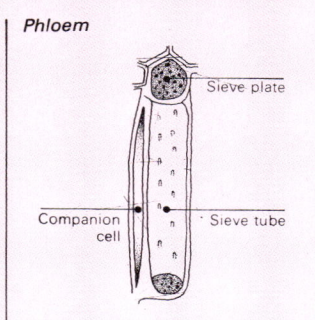

Parenchyma is a tissue that consists of thin-walled, many-sided cells. It is found in the central pith of stems, and in the cortex – the tissue that lies outside the XYLEM and PHLOEM of non-woody plants.

Phloem is the tissue that conducts food and other materials up and down the plant. Phloem tissue contains the conducting cells, or sieve tubes, together with companion cells, sclerenchyma fibres and parenchyma cells.

Plasma membrane. This cell membrane surrounds the cytoplasm. It is SEMI-PERMEABLE and lies just inside the cell wall.

Plasmodesmata are the protoplasmic connections between cells. Thin strands of cytoplasm pass through pores in the cell walls.

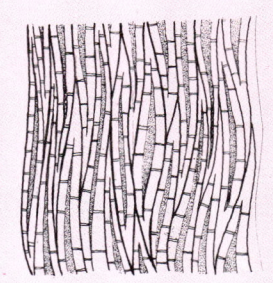

Proteins are complicated chemical compounds composed of long chains of AMINO ACIDS. *See* RNA.

Protoplasm consists of all the contents of a cell – including the CYTOPLASM and the NUCLEUS.

R RNA (Ribonucleic acid) is the chemical compound in the cell concerned with making proteins. It has the same basic structure as DNA, but it contains the base

How Plants Work

Above and left: The food materials made during photosynthesis are either stored in the leaf or transported via the phloem tissue to other parts of the plant. Respiration, which uses the products of photosynthesis, occurs in all parts of the plant. Oxygen for respiration is transported from the leaf via the phloem tissue. Carbon dioxide, the waste product of respiration, is transported back to the leaves and escapes via the stomata.

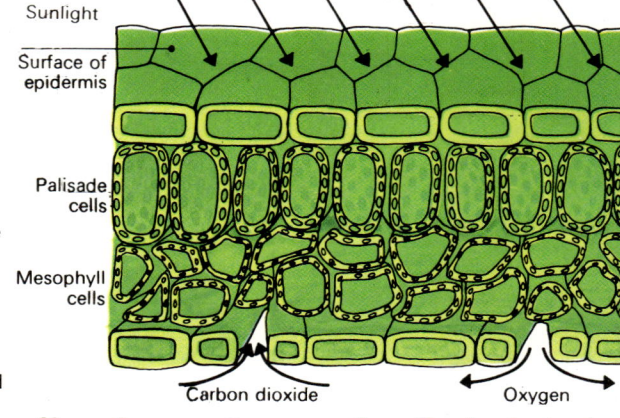

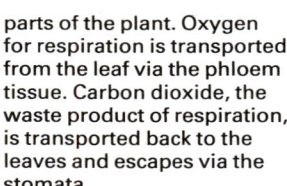

Above: A cross-section through a leaf. Carbon dioxide enters the leaf via the stomata and passes into the mesophyll cells via the air spaces that surround them. The dissolved carbon dioxide then diffuses into the palisade cells, which contain many chloroplasts. Here, photosynthesis takes place – assisted by sunlight.

Above: Deficiency or lack of a mineral may cause abnormalities in plants. This hop leaf has turned yellow due to a lack of a mineral needed to make chlorophyll. Lack of magnesium, an important element in chlorophyll, often leads to such yellowing.

Respiration can be regarded as the reverse of photosynthesis. Using oxygen from the air, sugar is chemically broken down by enzymes, and carbon dioxide, water and energy are released in the process. If there is not enough sugar present, some of the stored starch is converted back into sugar.

The energy released is stored in a compound called adenosine triphosphate (ATP). This is made by using the energy to add one phosphate group to adenosine diphosphate (ADP). ATP is a high energy compound. Its stored energy can be used to drive other chemical reactions. As it loses its energy, a phosphate group breaks off, and ADP is formed again.

During photosynthesis and respiration, oxygen, carbon and nitrogen are continuously being taken in and released by living organisms. There is thus a continuous cycle of events in which these elements are used.

Carbon is not used by itself, but is combined with oxygen to form carbon dioxide in the air. This is used by plants during photosynthesis to make CARBOHYDRATE chemicals, such as sugars, starch and cellulose. These are passed on to animals when the plants are eaten. Carbon dioxide is released back into the air in two ways. During respiration sugars are broken down to provide energy and carbon dioxide is given off in the process. Also, when plants and animals die, bacteria break down the carbohydrates into carbon dioxide and water.

uracil instead of thymine. Also, RNA molecules only consist of single strands. The 2 main forms of RNA concerned in protein synthesis are messenger RNA and transfer RNA. When a particular protein is to be made, a short strand of messenger RNA is formed by the DNA of the nucleus. This RNA contains certain 'orders' in the form of coded bases. The messenger RNA then moves into the cytoplasm, where it forms transfer RNA. This then picks up free AMINO ACIDS according to the 'orders' passed on by the messenger RNA. Meanwhile, the messenger RNA has positioned itself on the RIBOSOMES of the endoplasmic reticulum. The transfer RNA carries the amino acids to the messenger RNA, and the amino acids join up. The sequence in which the amino acids are joined together is controlled by the sequence of bases on the messenger RNA. Thus, the particular protein 'ordered' by the nucleus is made.

Ribosomes are granular bodies in the cytoplasm of a cell. Many ribosomes are attached to the surface of the ENDOPLASMIC RETICULUM. They are composed of RNA and protein and are made by the NUCLEOLUS. Sometimes they are linked together in long chains called polyribosomes. They are probably linked by a molecule of messenger RNA.

Root hairs are extensions of the epidermal cells of a root. The extension takes the form of a tube which grows out of the cell. Root hairs have very thin walls, and thus allow water to pass easily from the soil into the cells.

Root pressure is the pressure that causes water to pass from root cells into the XYLEM cells of the root. It is due to the fact that OSMOSIS occurs in the root cells. Differences in osmotic pressure

Stone cells

Sunlight in Wyre Forest

Oxygen in the air is used up during respiration. But plants also give off oxygen during photosynthesis. In fact, plants are essential for maintaining the oxygen content of the air.

Nitrogen is an extremely important element for living organisms. It is an essential part of AMINO ACIDS, which are the building blocks of proteins. There are large quantities (78 per cent) of nitrogen in the air, but unfortunately, this cannot be used by most plants. However, some organisms can 'fix' nitrogen and convert it directly into amino acids. In some cases these organisms have a symbiotic relationship with plant roots which is mutually beneficial. For example, the root nodules of pea plants contain a bacterium called *Rhizobium* which can 'fix' nitrogen inside the root nodules.

All the other elements that plants need are obtained as minerals from the soil. In addition to nitrogen, the most important elements are potassium, calcium, phosphorus, magnesium, sulphur and iron. Although they are essential, they are only needed in small quantities. For example, the solid parts of a plant (i.e. excluding the water) only contain about three and a half per cent potassium. But without potassium a plant cannot survive.

Other elements, called trace elements, are needed in even smaller quantities — less than 0.0001 per cent. These are copper, manganese, zinc, molybdenum and boron. Even so they are still essential. For example, lack of zinc causes the leaves of a plant to become deformed.

Plant pigments

The countryside is largely green, and this is due

Below: Oxygen, carbon and nitrogen are continually being recycled. Carbon is present as carbon dioxide in the air and as the many carbon compounds that make up the bodies of animals and plants. Carbon dioxide is taken up during photosynthesis. It is released during respiration, when plants and animals die and decompose, and when fuels are burned. Oxygen in the air is used up during respiration and burning, and is given off during photosynthesis. Nitrogen is mostly taken up by plants in the form of nitrates, although some bacteria can 'fix' nitrogen directly from the air.

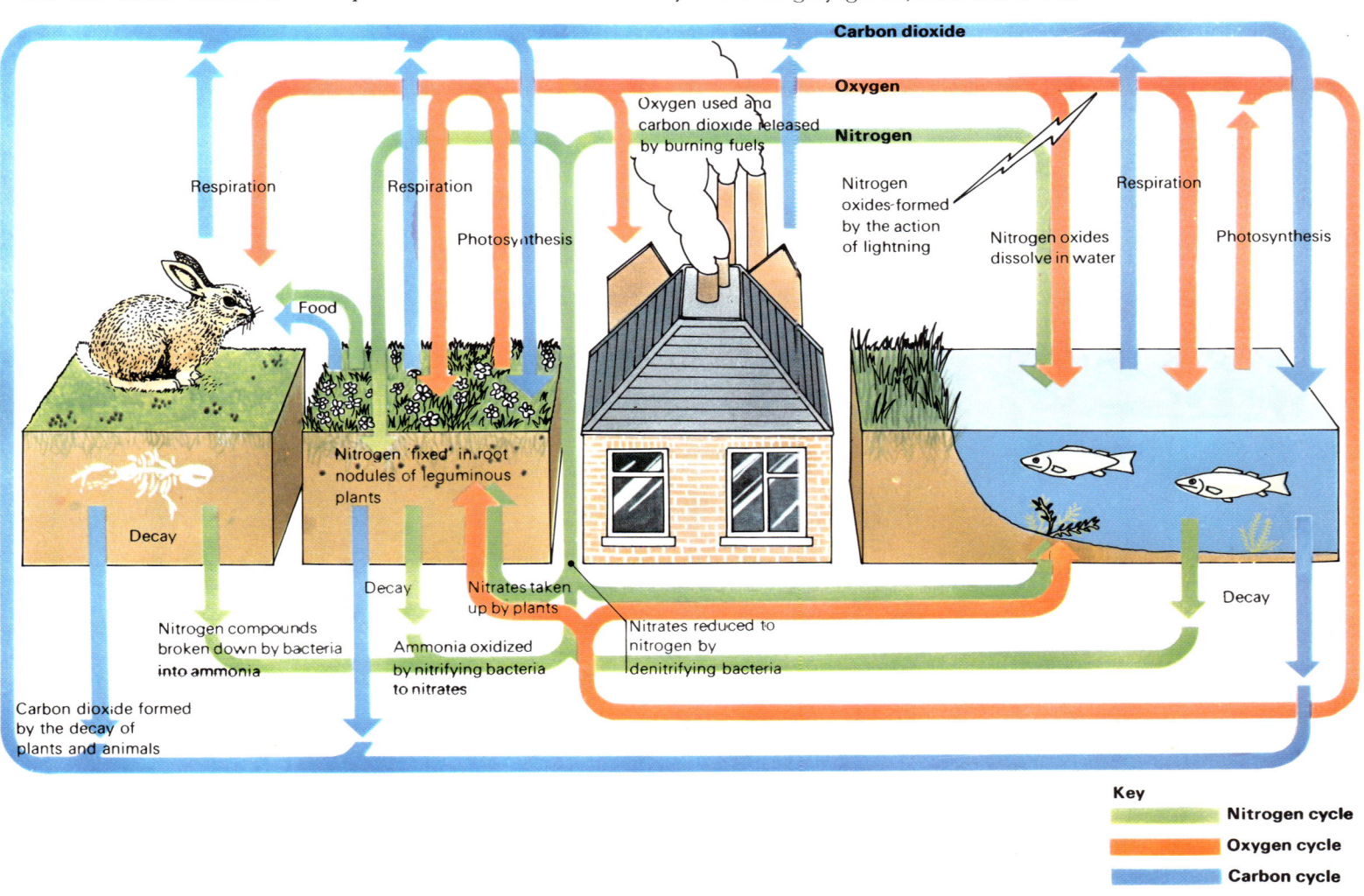

---

are maintained by ions being actively transported by a special mechanism across cell membranes. When transpiration is slow, root pressure may cause the phenomenon of guttation. Water exudes through special glands on the edges of leaves.

Sclerenchyma is a tissue that consists of stiff, non-living cells, heavily thickened with cellulose, lignin, or both. Sclerenchyma fibres are long, thin cells, pointed at both ends. They are found in many parts of plants. The cellulose fibres of the flax plant (*Linum usitatissimum*) are used for making linen, and the lignified fibres of hemp (*Cannabis sativa*) are used for making rope.

Semi-permeable membrane is a membrane that allows some substances to diffuse through it but not others. The plasma membrane of a cell is a semi-permeable membrane that allows water to pass through, but not substances such as mineral ions and proteins dissolved in water.

Starch is a CARBOHYDRATE. It is also a polysaccharide, i.e. its molecules are made up of many sugar units. Starch is the main food storage compound used by plants. It is found in large quantities in seeds and storage organs such as potato tubers.

Stomata (*singular:* stoma) are the 'breathing pores' on the undersides of the leaves of plants. A stoma consists of 2 guard cells that are shaped like kidneys. By altering the TURGOR PRESSURE inside the guard cells, the plant can open or close them. Carbon dioxide and oxygen pass in and out of the stomata during photosynthesis and respiration. During transpiration, water is lost by evaporation from the stomata.

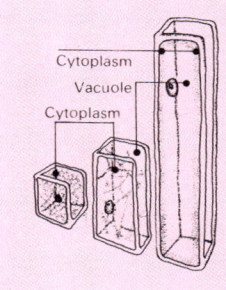

Vacuole

Antirrhinum

to the chlorophyll pigment present in most plants. But there are also other plant pigments, and some of these give us the other brilliant colours of nature.

The xanthophylls and carotenes are a group of pigments ranging in colour from yellows to reds. Like chlorophyll they are photosynthetic pigments and are found in the leaves. In the autumn the chlorophyll of a deciduous tree is withdrawn from the leaves. The xanthophylls and carotenes that remain give the leaves their familiar yellow-brown autumn colour. The same pigments give the colour to apples, carrots, tomatoes and brown algae.

The anthocyanin pigments provide the most spectacular of the plant colours — the bright violets, blues and reds. They are mostly found in flowers, but some fruits also contain anthocyanins.

The last group of pigments are phycoerythrin and phycocyanin. They only occur in certain groups of algae, such as the blue-green algae and the red algae.

Below: The reds, browns and yellows of autumn leaves are due to the presence of xanthophylls and carotenes.

Above: The brilliant blue colour of gentian violets is due to the presence of one of the anthocyanin pigments.

Right: The familiar bright yellow colour of daffodils is produced by xanthophyll and carotene pigments.

Stone cells, or sclereids, are irregularly shaped cells. They are common in seed coats and fruits, such as pears and nuts.

Suberin is a waterproof substance made up of a number of carbon compounds. It is found in the walls of cork cells. The chemicals involved in suberin are all formed from compounds called fatty acids.

Suction pressure is the capacity of a cell to take in water. It is equal to the OSMOTIC PRESSURE less the TURGOR PRESSURE. Suction pressure is not an active force of the cell. Water is pushed rather than sucked in. Inside a plant, water moves from one cell to another until the concentration of water in the cells is equal.

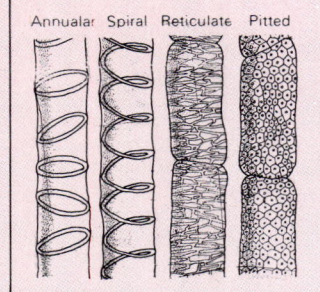

Sugars are carbohydrates that have a sweet taste. They are divided into 2 groups. Monosaccharides are the simple sugars whose molecules have 5 or 6 carbon atoms. Examples include ribose, an important constituent of DNA and RNA, and glucose, which is made by plants during photosynthesis. Disaccharides are sugars whose molecules are made up of 2 monosaccharide molecules. An example is sucrose.

T Transpiration is the loss of water by evaporation from the stomata of a plant. Some water is also lost through the cuticle of the epidermis.

Transpiration stream covers the flow of water from the ROOT HAIRS, through the XYLEM vessels, to the STOMATA of a plant.

Turgor pressure (wall pressure) is the pressure exerted by the cell wall that tends to prevent water entering the cell by OSMOSIS. Turgor is a term used to describe the state of the cell when the cell wall is stretched as far as possible.

V Vacuole. This is the fluid-filled space enclosed by the cytoplasm of the cell. Its presence is due to the fact that when cells grow, the amount of cytoplasm does not increase, so it becomes stretched round the inside of the cell wall.

X Xylem is the tissue that conducts water and minerals up the plant. It consists of xylem vessels, or tracheids, SCLERENCHYMA fibres, and PARENCHYMA cells.

Xylem
Annualar Spiral Reticulate Pitted

We often associate bacteria with disease, but they also perform the vital role of breaking down all dead organisms. Bacteria and many algae are microscopic, single-celled plants, but algae also include giant seaweeds.

Bacteria and Algae

Right: Some forms of bacteria.
1. Bacilli have rod-shaped cells. **2.** Cocci have spherical cells. Some cocci occur in clusters, such as *Staphylococcus*. **3.** Spirillar bacteria have curved or twisted rod-shaped cells, often with flagella. **4.** *Streptococcus* has long chains of spherical cells.

Below: Bacteria are used in the making of cheeses. One type of bacterium begins the process by causing the milk to curdle. Other types of bacteria make acid or digest fats or proteins. Different types of cheese are made by varying the extent to which each type of bacterium plays a part.

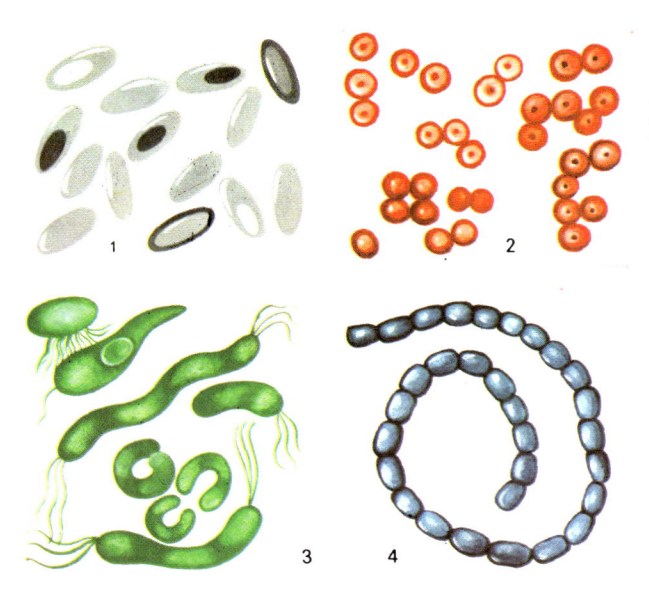

Bacteria are minute single-celled organisms. Many scientists include them in the plant kingdom, but they are not like other plants. Their cells have no nuclei, and their cell walls are not made of cellulose. Instead, they are made up of a number of substances, including proteins and fats. Some bacteria can move, others cannot. Some need oxygen to survive, but others are poisoned by oxygen.

A few bacteria make their own food by photosynthesis, but most of them live by breaking down dead plant and animal material. Such bacteria are essential for life to continue. When they break down materials, they make simple chemicals that can be used again by other plants. Thus, there is no waste in the living world.

Some of these bacteria are particularly useful to us. In the treatment of sewage, bacteria are allowed to act on the raw sewage and make it harmless. We also use bacteria to make silage and garden compost by rotting down plant material.

Some plants and animals use bacteria more directly. Many plant-eating animals, such as rabbits, horses and cows, have bacteria in their digestive systems. The presence of these bacteria is essential for the breakdown and digestion of cellulose, which the animals cannot do by themselves. Some flowering plants, such as clover and other members of the pea family, have bacteria in their roots. These bacteria help the plants by converting, or fixing, nitrogen into a form that plants can use.

Many bacteria have less desirable effects. For example, they cause food to decay. Also, the presence of some bacteria in food causes food poisoning. Many other diseases, such as typhoid fever, tuberculosis and cholera are caused by bacteria. Plants, too, may be infected, as for instance, soft rot in carrots and fire blight in

Reference

A **Anisogamy** is a type of sexual reproduction in which 2 unalike sex cells (gametes) fuse. The larger of the 2 cells (the 'female') is able to move by means of one or more FLAGELLA. See also ISOGAMY, OOGAMY.
Antheridium. This is the male sex organ of a lower plant, e.g. some brown algae, the liverworts, mosses and ferns. Inside an antheridium the male sex cells, or antherozoids, are formed.
Asexual reproduction is the way in which an organism reproduces itself without involving sex cells.

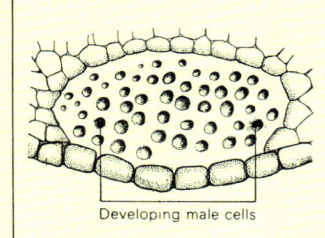

Antheridium

B **Bacillariophytes**, see DIATOMS.
Bacteria are a group of single-celled organisms that have no definite nucleus (their DNA is distributed throughout their cells), and no chlorophyll. They are usually classified as plants, but sometimes they are put into a third kingdom, Protista, which includes the protozoa (single-celled animals), single-celled algae and fungi.

C **Chlamydomonas** is a genus of single-celled algae belonging to the

Diatoms

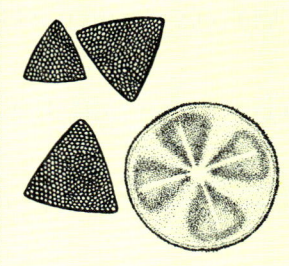

Chlorophytes. Members of this genus have 2 flagella. Most of the cell is occupied by a single, basin-shaped chloroplast.
Chrysophytes are a group of single-celled, or colonial, algae. They are golden brown.
Cyanophytes are the blue-green algae. They have no definite nuclei (their DNA is distributed throughout their cells). They exist in both single-celled and filamentous forms, and they are mostly found in fresh water. They contain chlorophyll and phycoerythrin and phycobilin. These pigments give them their characteristic blue-green colour.

D **Decay**, see PUTREFACTION.

18 Bacteria and Algae

pears. These diseases are slowly disappearing.

The closest relatives of the bacteria are the blue-green algae. Like bacteria they do not have cellulose cell walls, and their cells do not have definite nuclei. In addition, many blue-green algae are able to fix nitrogen. However, blue-green algae have one main thing in common with other plants. they contain chlorophyll and can therefore make their own food.

Most blue-green algae are composed of strings, or filaments, of cells. These are surrounded by a slimy material called mucilage. Blue-green algae live in ponds and streams, in the sea, and even in hot springs. Sometimes they cause problems by growing in drinking water supplies.

Algae

Algae vary from single-celled plants to large many-celled seaweeds. At first glance, such plants would seem to have little in common. However, they are all simple plants with no roots or stems, and they all live permanently in water, between the high and low tide marks, or on damp walls and trees.

Many single-celled algae float freely in the water, together with many tiny animals. This drifting mass of minute animals and plants is called plankton. The animals (zooplankton) feed on the plants (phytoplankton), and both are eaten by larger plankton-eating animals, such as fish and whales.

Among the single-celled algae are simple round forms, such as *Pleurococcus*, which grows on damp tree trunks. Other single-celled algae have complicated shapes, such as *Ceratium*, an algae that lives in the sea. The DIATOMS are a group of algae that have silica in their cell walls. Many

Left: During the process of sewage treatment bacteria are used to destroy the waste matter. Air is bubbled through the sewage to provide the oxygen necessary for this.

Right: Some forms of algae. *Euglena* is a green alga that swims by using its whip-like hair, or flagellum. *Nostoc* is a blue-green alga. Its long chains of cells are contained within a slimy sheath. *Coscinodiscus* is a diatom. Its hard cell wall is made of silica and is made in 2 parts – like a pill box. *Cladophora* is a branched filamentous alga. *Fucus* is a brown alga, familiar as the seaweed found on many shores.

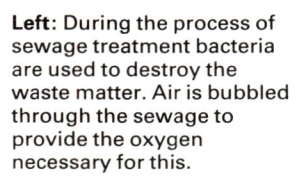

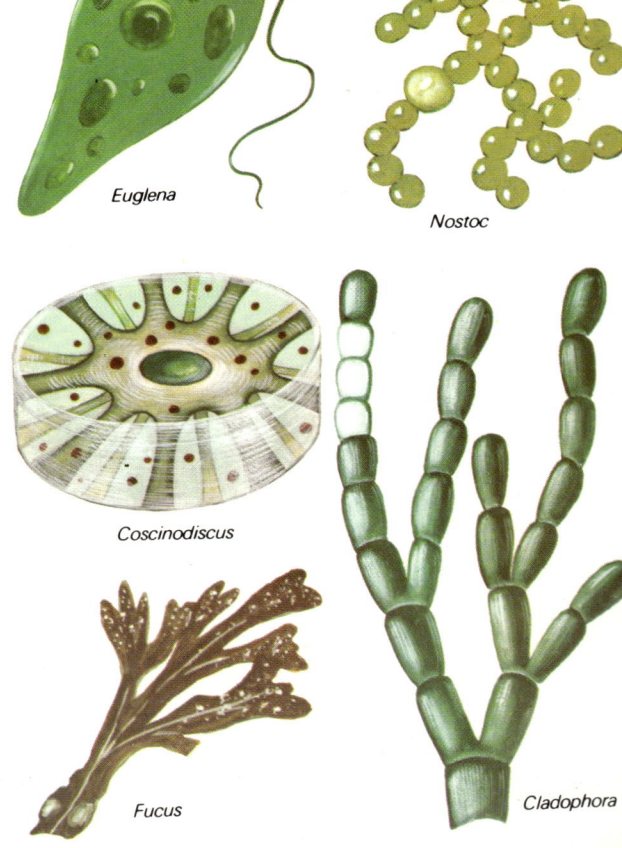

Euglena

Nostoc

Coscinodiscus

Fucus

Cladophora

Diatoms are a group of single-celled algae, also known as Bacillariophytes. They have cell walls that contain silica, and they are golden brown in colour.

E **Euglena** is a genus of single-celled algae belonging to the Euglenophyta. Members of this genus have a long flagellum that emerges from a gullet at the front end of the cell. A disk – or star-shaped chloroplast is also present, and thus *Euglena* species make their own food by photosynthesis. Individuals that grow in the dark lose their chloroplasts and feed by taking in organic material – i.e. in the same way as animals.

Euglenophytes are a group of single-celled algae. They have 1, 2 or 3 flagella. They are green in colour and are generally regarded as plants. However, they do have some animal characteristics (see EUGLENA).

F **Fertilization** is the fusion of 2 sex cells. The cell that results from this fusion is called a zygote.
Flagellum (*plural:* flagella) is a whip-like organ possessed by algae and protozoans (single-celled animals). By lashing its flagellum an organism is able to swim through the water.

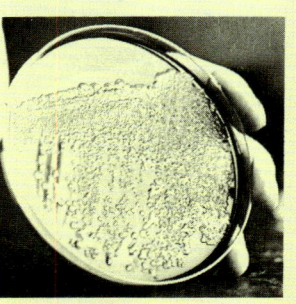

Bacteria culture

Food poisoning occurs when certain chemicals or bacteria are eaten with food. Bacteria that cause food poisoning include salmonellae, staphylococci and clostridia.
Fucus is a genus of brown seaweeds belonging to the Phaeophytes. There are several well-known species, including *F. vesiculosus* (bladder wrack), *F. serratus* (serrated wrack) and *F. spiralis* (twisted wrack).

G **Gametes** are sex cells. During the process of sexual reproduction 2 ga-

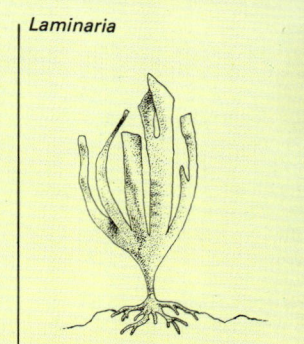

Laminaria

metes fuse to form a zygote.

I **Isogamy** is a type of sexual reproduction in

Bacteria and Algae

diatoms, too, have beautifully sculpted shapes. A large number of algae, such as CHLAMYDOMONAS and EUGLENA, have whip-like organs called flagella. By using these they are able to move from place to place — usually a characteristic of animals. In fact, scientists have argued about whether *Euglena* is a plant or an animal, as it not only has a flagellum, but also has other animal-like characteristics.

The simplest type of many-celled alga is called a colony. This is just a group of cells that all work together. For example, *Volvox* consists of a round, hollow ball of cells; each cell is like a single *Chlamydomonas* individual.

Many algae consist of long filaments (threads) of cells joined end to end. The simplest of these include ULOTHRIX and SPIROGYRA, which both have long, unbranched filaments. More complicated types have branched filaments. *Cladophora* has a tree-like system of branches, and it is anchored to the ground by a tiny root-like structure. *Stigeoclonium* has two sets of branches. One reaches upwards like a tree; the other spreads over the ground.

Most of these algae can only be seen clearly with a microscope, but there are a number of larger types. The STONEWORTS, such as *Chara*, are a freshwater group that resemble higher plants. They have 'stems' with rings of 'branches' around them. Most of the larger algae grow in the sea, and we know them as seaweeds. SEA LETTUCE is a green seaweed that consists of a flat

Below: Some tropical species of oarweeds may reach 200 metres in length. They are anchored to the rocks by holdfasts or root substitutes.

Above: The green colour of the bark of this beech tree is due to the presence of the round, single-celled, green alga *Pleurococcus*.

Below: *Volvox* is a colonial green alga in which many cells are arranged to form a hollow ball. These 4 colonies each have daughter colonies inside.

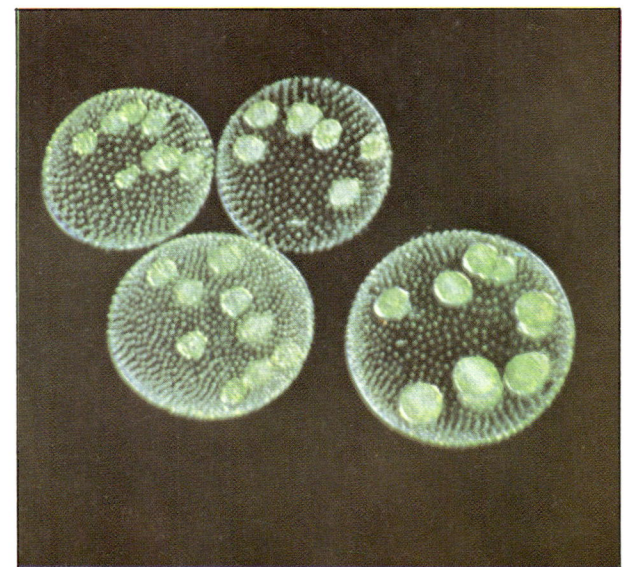

---

which 2 identical sex cells (gametes) fuse. *See also* ANISOGAMY, OOGAMY.

L **Laminaria** is a genus of brown seaweeds belonging to the PHAEOPHYTES. They have large flattened fronds. Because of their appearance, they are often called oar weeds.

N **Nitrogen-fixing bacteria** are those that can convert nitrogen into nitrogen-containing salts that can be used by plants. They include *Rhizobium* which is found in the root nodules of leguminous plants, and *Azotobacter*, which lives free in the soil.

O **Oogamy** is a type of sexual reproduction in which a swimming male sex cell (antherozoid) fuses with a large, stationary female sex cell (oosphere).

Oogonium is the female sex organ of some brown algae and fungi. Inside an oogonium, one or more female sex cells, or oospheres, are formed.

P **Phaeophytes** are a group of brown sea algae. Most of them, including FUCUS and LAMINARIA, grow in-between the high and low tide marks.

Pleurococcus is a genus of

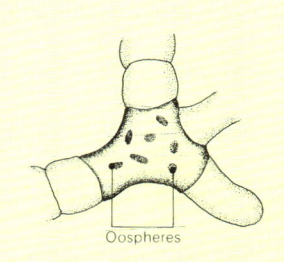

Oogonium

algae belonging to the CHLOROPHYTES. It is one of the simplest algae, consisting of a single round cell without any flagella. Its only method of reproduction is by simple division.

Putrefaction is the decomposition by BACTERIA of plant or animal material that contains protein. During this process the proteins are broken down into various foul-smelling chemicals.

Pyrrophytes are a group of single-celled algae that range in colour from yellow through green to dark brown. This group includes

Sea lettuce

the dinoflagellates, which often glow in the sea.

R **Rhodophytes** are a group of red algae. They

Bacteria and Algae

sheet of cells. Red seaweeds (RHODOPHYTES) often grow to over 30 centimetres in length. Many of them consist of a complicated and delicate cell arrangement. However, the brown seaweeds are probably the most familiar. This group includes the largest of all the algae; some of them can be over 100 metres long. They include the wracks and kelps. Many of these anchor themselves to the rock by structures called holdfasts. Some seaweeds float freely.

How algae reproduce

The simplest forms of reproduction do not involve any sex cells. If parts of a filamentous algae break off, they continue to grow and thus form new individuals. Many single-celled algae reproduce by simply dividing into two. A more complicated type of asexual ('without sex') reproduction involves the formation of swimming cells called zoospores. When these are released, they can swim to a new site and then grow.

Sexual reproduction involves sex cells. Some algae produce only one kind of swimming sex cell. In such cases the two identical sex cells fuse together, and the resulting cell, or zygote, grows into a new plant. A slightly more advanced form of sexual reproduction occurs when unlike sex cells are formed. The larger of the two (the 'female') swims to meet the smaller sex cell (the 'male') with which it then fuses.

The most advanced type of reproduction found in the algae involves a swimming male sex cell, called an antherozoid, and a large, non-swimming female sex cell, called an oosphere. Antherozoids are produced in a special sex organ called an antheridium. An oosphere is produced in an oogonium. The antherozoids swim to the oosphere and fusion, or fertilization, takes place inside the oogonium. The zygote is released and eventually grows into a new plant.

Right: Asexual reproduction in *Spirogyra* simply involves breaking the filament. New cells are then added on to the 2 halves by mitosis.

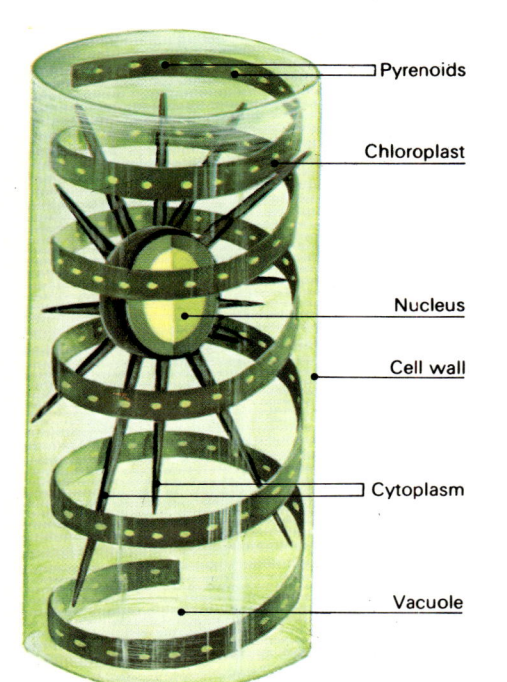

Below: A single cell of the filamentous alga *Spirogyra*. Its spiral chloroplast is unique to the plant kingdom.

Pyrenoids
Chloroplast
Nucleus
Cell wall
Cytoplasm
Vacuole

Above: Sexual reproduction, or conjugation in *Spirogyra*.
1. Cells of neighbouring filaments produce outgrowths. 2. The outgrowths join to form a tunnel. 3. One nucleus begins to migrate through the tunnel. 4. The 2 nuclei fuse. 5. A zygote is formed.

Below: In asexual reproduction of *Chlamydomonas* (top), an individual simply divides into 2 inside its cell wall. Sexual reproduction in *Chlamydomonas* (bottom) involves the formation of sex cells.

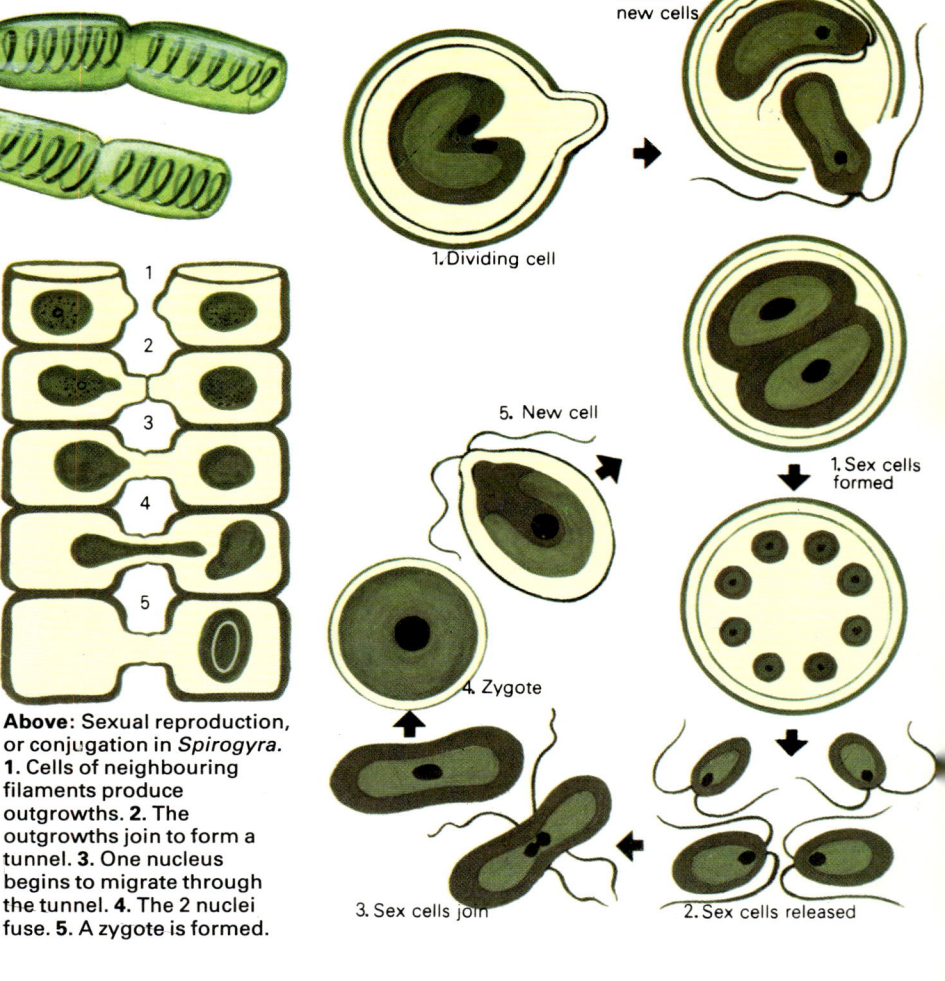

1. Dividing cell
2. Two new cells
5. New cell
4. Zygote
3. Sex cells join
1. Sex cells formed
2. Sex cells released

---

are many-celled and often have delicate shapes. They mostly grow in the sea, and their red colour is due to pigments that allow photosynthesis to occur in deep water where the light is dim.

S **Sea lettuce** (*Ulva lactuca*) is a species of algae belonging to the CHLOROPHYTES. It grows in the sea, between high and low tide marks, and it consists of a flat sheet of cells attached to a rock by a short stalk.
Sexual reproduction is the way in which an organism reproduces itself when sex cells (gametes) are involved.
Spirogyra is a genus of

Clover plant with root nodules

algae belonging to the CHLOROPHYTES. They are un-branched, filamentous algae that grow in fresh water. Each cell has an unusual chloroplast which forms a spiral that runs the length of the cell.
Stigeoclonium is a genus of algae belonging to the CHLOROPHYTES. They are branched, filamentous algae, and each branch ends in a tapering cell.
Stoneworts are a group of green algae that are totally unlike any other group. They have distinct 'stems', and at intervals along the stems

they have rings of small 'branches'. There are only 8 types of stonewort, all of which are found in fresh water; the 2 most common are *Chara* and *Nitella*.

U **Ulothrix** is a genus of algae belonging to the Chlorophytes. They are un-branched, filamentous algae, with ring-shaped chloroplasts in their cells.
Ulva lactuca, see SEA LETTUCE.

V **Volvox** is a genus of colonial algae belonging to the Chlorophytes group.

They consist of hollow balls of CHLAMYDOMONAS-like cells.

W **Wracks,** see FUCUS.

X **Xanthophytes** are a group of algae that are yellow-green in colour. They are mostly single-celled plants that grow in fresh water or in damp soil.

Z **Zygote,** see FERTILIZATION.

The familiar mushroom and the tiny pin mould on stale bread belong to the same large division within the plant kingdom – the fungi. Sometimes a fungus lives in a strange partnership with algae, which is called a lichen.

Fungi and Lichens

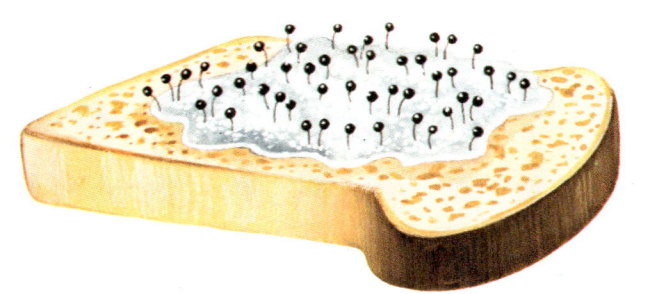

Above: *Mucor*, the pin mould, is often found growing on stale bread. The name pin mould comes from the pin-like structures called sporangia that contain the asexual spores.
Left: The sexual reproduction of *Mucor* involves nuclei from 2 separate hyphae (threads). They fuse and a tough zygospore is formed. When conditions are right this germinates to form a new mass of hyphae, or mycelium.

Above: Potato blight is a disease caused by the fungus *Phytophathora infestans*. The fungus attacks the stem and leaves causing them to die.

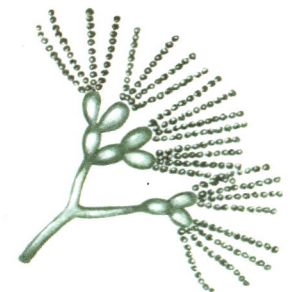

Above: *Penicillium* is a fungus that produces long chains of asexual spores, or conidia.

Fungi are plants that do not contain chlorophyll (green pigment). As a result they cannot make their own food; they have to use sources of ready-made food. There are over 50,000 kinds of fungi, and they include the moulds, rusts, yeasts and toadstools, as well as several other groups.

Some fungi live on decaying plant or animal tissue. They are called saprophytes and they produce enzymes that break down the chemicals of the tissue. The fungi can then absorb the broken down chemicals. Other fungi are parasites – that is they live on other organisms without benefiting their hosts in any way. Some parasites do not harm their hosts, but others destroy their hosts completely.

A few fungi are single-celled, but most of them have a plant body called a mycelium, which is made up of long threads, or hyphae. There are three main groups of fungi, and the main difference between them is in the way that the members of each group reproduce.

Phycomycetes – simple fungi

The simplest fungi include the PIN MOULDS, downy mildews and potato blight. Species of pin mould can often be found growing on stale bread and other foods. The mycelium spreads over the surface of the food and produces upright branches with tiny pin heads. These heads are spore-containers called sporangia. Pin moulds also have a form of sexual reproduction. Two chemically different hyphae produce outgrowths that join up to produce a hard black object called a zygospore. From this grows a single thread, which produces a sporangium at the tip.

Downy mildews are parasites, and various

Reference

A **Agaricus** is a genus of TOADSTOOLS that includes the edible field mushroom (*A. campestris*), cultivated mushroom (*A. bisporus*), and horse mushroom (*A. arvensis*). The yellow stainer (*A. xanthoderma*) is a poisonous fungus. It can be distinguished by its vivid yellow flesh at the base of the STIPE and by its unpleasant carbolic smell.
Amanita is a genus of toadstools, most of which are poisonous or inedible. The most poisonous is the death cap (*A. phalloides*), which has a greenish cap and white gills. The fly agaric (*A. muscaria*), with its scarlet, white-flecked cap is also poisonous. However, it is not usually fatal. Some species of *Amanita* are edible, such as the blusher (*A. rubescens*), which has a brown cap with white flecks. Its flesh turns pink when bruised. Great care must be taken to distinguish it from the poisonous panther cap (*A. pantherina*), which has a greenish cap.
Annulus. This is the membranous ring near the top of the STIPE of a toadstool. It is the remains of the membrane that joined the edge of the cap to the stipe while the toadstool was developing.
Ascomycetes are fungi whose hyphae are divided into cells with many nuclei by crosswalls, and whose spores are produced in asci (*see below*). They include YEASTS and MOREL.
Ascus (*plural*: asci). This is a round, cylindrical or club-shaped cell in which spores (normally 8) are formed during the sexual reproduction of ascomycetes.

B **Basidiomycetes** are fungi whose hyphae are divided into cells with many

Blusher

nuclei by crosswalls, and whose spores are produced on basidia (*see below*). They include the familiar types of MUSHROOMS and TOADSTOOLS.
Basidium (*plural:* basidia) is a cylindrical or club-shaped cell in which 2 or 4 spores are formed during the sexual reproduction of basidiomycetes. The ripe spores are borne outside the basidium on small projections called sterigmata.
Boletus is a large genus of toadstools that produce their basidia in pores. Also known as ceps, they are nearly all edible. The most common

Right: A rust fungus on the leaves of coltsfoot. The rust-red patches are where the spores of the fungus are produced.
Left: The fruiting body of a Morel *(Morchella esculenta)*. This is an edible fungus that grows on rich soil in spring. It is an ascomycete and its spores are produced in the hollows on the 'cap'.

species attack a number of flowering plants, including onions, cabbages, tobacco and maize. The fungus grows in the spaces between the cells of the host, and inside the cells it produces club-shaped organs that absorb food from the host.

POTATO BLIGHT is a serious disease of potatoes. During the winter it lives inside potato tubers. In the spring the mycelium grows into the potato shoots and can completely ruin a potato crop. The fungus is spread by spores, which are produced on the surface of the leaves of an infected host plant.

Ascomycetes – more advanced fungi

Ascomycetes get their name from the fact that during sexual reproduction they produce spores in structures called asci (see ASCUS). Many ascomycetes produce their asci in fruiting bodies that can be seen without a microscope. *Peziza* has a cup-shaped fruiting body. Morels have large, stalked fruiting bodies.

Many ascomycetes are parasites, and their fruiting bodies are small. The powdery mildews attack a wide range of plants, including gooseberry bushes, strawberry plants, oak trees and chrysanthemums. They produce round fruiting bodies in which the asci are completely enclosed.

The ERGOT OF RYE is a parasite that has flask-shaped fruiting bodies. These grow from small, black masses of hyphae, called ergots, which replace some of the grains of rye. Ergots can be used to produce the drug ergotin, which is used to stop bleeding. If they are ground up into flour with the rest of the grain, they can cause a serious disease in man and animals called ergotism.

Some ascomycetes are single-celled fungi. The alcohol-producing yeasts are examples of this type. Like other ascomycetes they can reproduce by forming asci, but they mainly reproduce by budding. Each cell divides into two, and in this way the fungus grows long chains of cells. These fungi can live on sugar and convert it into ethyl alcohol and carbon dioxide, and they are therefore used in the fermentation of wines and beers. Other single-celled ascomycetes include peach leaf curl and Dutch elm disease.

Many species of PENICILLIUM, the fungus from which we get penicillin, do not produce asci – or at least they have never been discovered. However, we know that they are ascomycetes because of the detailed structure of their mycelia. *Penicillium* produces asexual spores called conidia on the head of a club-shaped structure called a conidiophore. There are several ascomycetes whose asci have not yet been discovered, and they are often classed in a separate group called the *Fungi Imperfecti*.

Above: *Helvella lacunosa* is a woodland fungus that produces its fruiting bodies in autumn. It is an ascomycete and its spores are formed on the grey 'cap'.

Basidiomycetes – the most advanced fungi

Basidiomycetes produce spores on structures called basidia (see BASIDIUM). Many basidiomycetes have large fruiting bodies, and this group includes the MUSHROOMS and TOADSTOOLS.

The rusts and smuts are parasitic basidiomy-

---

species is *B. edulis* which has a brown cap and greenish-yellow pores. The only poisonous species is the devil's boletus (*B. satanus*), which can easily be recognized by its red pores and stipe.

C Chanterelle (*Cantherellus cibarius*) is a funnel-shaped toadstool that is egg-yolk yellow in colour and has a faint smell of apricots. It grows in all woods in summer and autumn. It is difficult to find, but this excellently flavoured fungus is worth looking for.

Coprinus is a large genus of toadstools that includes the ink caps. The easiest to identify is the shaggy ink cap (*C. comatus*), which has a tall, white, shaggy cap and pink gills that turn black and disintegrate as the spores ripen. It is edible, but only the young fruiting bodies are recommended.

D Death cap, see AMANITA.
Dry rot (*Merulius lacrymans*) is a soft, jelly-like fungus that lives on wood. It needs damp conditions in order to start growing, but once established it can make water from organic chemicals. It has thick, water-conducting hyphae and it can penetrate brick and stone in order to reach more wood supplies.

E Ergot of rye (*Claviceps purpurea*) is a parasitic ASCOMYCETE that replaces the grains of rye with small, black ergots. It also attacks other grasses.

F Fairy ring champignon (*Marasmius oreades*). A small toadstool that forms clumps and rings in grassland. It is beige in colour, with a slightly pointed cap, and well separated gills. It is edible, and is recommended for drying.
Fly agaric, see AMANITA.

G Giant puff ball (*Calvitia gigantea*). A large, white, round fungus that grows in grassland. It may

Common puff balls

cetes with relatively small fruiting bodies. They cause serious diseases in grain crops, such as wheat, barley, oats and maize.

The jelly fungi, such as the JEW'S EAR FUNGUS, have soft, clammy fruiting bodies, usually attached to trees. Some of them are parasites and grow on living trees, others are saprophytes and grow on dead wood.

Another group of basidiomycetes produce their spores in an enclosed fruiting body, which only opens when the spores are ripe. These include puff balls and giant puff balls. The STINKHORN is a special member of this group.

Toadstools and bracket fungi are a familiar sight in fields and woods. What you see is only the fruiting body; the main body of the fungus, the mycelium, is in the soil or wood from which the fruiting body is growing.

A toadstool consists of a stalk and an umbrella-shaped cap. The underside of the cap may be covered with gills that radiate outwards like the spokes of a wheel. These are lined with spore-bearing basidia. Some toadstools have pores lined with basidia, and a few types have spines instead of gills. Bracket fungi are similar

Left: The fly agaric *(Amanita muscaria)* is a colourful, but poisonous, toadstool found in pine and birch woods in autumn.

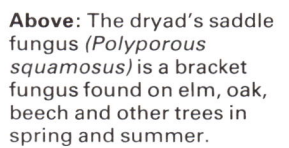

Above: The dryad's saddle fungus *(Polyporous squamosus)* is a bracket fungus found on elm, oak, beech and other trees in spring and summer.

Below: The orange peel fungus *(Peziza aurantia)* is an ascomycete cup fungus. Its spores are produced inside the cups.

---

grow larger than a man's head, and it is sometimes known as the *Tête de mort* (head of death). It is edible, and is best fried.

Honey fungus *(Armillaria mellea)* is a parasitic fungus that produces toadstools at the base of its host tree. It can be a serious parasite of fruit trees, but the toadstools are good to eat.

Ink caps, see COPRINUS.

Jew's ear fungus *(Auricularia auricula).* This is a jelly fungus with brownish-purple, wrinkled fruiting bodies that sometimes resemble ears. In Britain it is found on elder trees.

Honey fungus

Lichens are symbiotic associations of algae and fungi. A typical lichen consists of 3 layers. The upper layer is made up of densely interwoven fungal hyphae, forming an almost solid tissue. In the middle layer the fungal hyphae are more loosely interwoven. In the upper part of this layer are scattered groups of algal cells. The lower layer again consists of a mass of fungal hyphae, and small, root-like hyphae project from the lower surface. These hold the lichen firmly onto the rock or bark.

Morel *(Morchella esculenta)* is a stalked ASCOMYCETE. The surface of the

Cladonia (lichen)

'cap' is covered in small ridges, which separate many pits. The spores are formed in these pits. Morels are excellent to eat.

Mucor, see PIN MOULD.

Mushroom is a name used to describe the fruiting bodies of a number of BASIDIOMYCETES and a few ASCOMYCETES (e.g. morels). However, it is most commonly used to describe the fruiting bodies of the edible species of AGARICUS, such as the field mushroom. There is no clear distinction between a mushroom and a TOADSTOOL.

Fungi and Lichens

Parasol mushroom

Devil's boletus

Death cap

Boletus edulis (Cep)

Oyster fungus

Shaggy ink cap

Giant puff ball

Chanterelle

Sulphur tuft

Above: The fruiting bodies, or toadstools, of several basidiomycete fungi. The parasol mushroom, cep (*B. edulis*), giant puff ball and chanterelle make excellent food. The oyster mushroom and shaggy ink cap are also edible, but their quality is only moderate. The devils boletus and the death cap are extremely poisonous. The sulphur tuft is also poisonous.

Below: In suitable conditions mushroom spores germinate to produce a mycelium. A fruiting body begins as a small round swelling that grows rapidly. When it emerges above the ground the cap and stipe have developed. As the spores ripen the edge of the cap breaks away, exposing the gills, and leaving a ring called the annulus.

Cap — Gills — Annulus — Stipe

Spores

O **Oyster mushroom** (*Pleurotus ostreatus*) is an edible bracket fungus found on beech and other trees. The upper surface is bluish-grey when the fruiting body is young, but turns brown as it gets older.

P **Parasite** is an organism that lives on another organism (the host) from which it obtains food. The host does not benefit, and in some cases may be destroyed. There are many parasitic fungi, such as HONEY FUNGUS and POTATO BLIGHT.

Parasol mushroom (*Lepiota procera*) is an edible toadstool that grows in grassy clearings or at the edges of woods. The cap is light brown and is covered in brown scales. The stipe is striped brown and has a loose, double collar-like ring. The shaggy parasol (*L. rhacodes*) is also edible. It is similar to the parasol mushroom, but it has a smooth stipe without stripes.

Penicillium is a genus of ASCOMYCETES. Some species cause disease in weak or dormant parts of plants, such as over-ripe fruits and bulbs. Others are used to make antibiotics, such as pencillin. Many are used in cheese, such as *P. roqueforti* and *P. camemberti*.

Phycomycetes are fungi

Young parasol mushrooms

whose hyphae do not have crosswalls. These include the PIN MOULDS.

Pin moulds (*Mucor*) are a genus of phycomycetes most of which are SAPROPHYTES. The name is derived from their pin-like structures in which asexual spores are produced.

Polyporus is a genus of bracket fungi that produce their basidia in pores. There are many species, including the dryad's saddle (*P. squamosus*), which is an edible fungus.

Potato blight (*Phytophthora infestans*) is a species of phycomycetes that cause late blight in potatoes. It can be controlled by spraying the plants with Bordeaux mixture, which includes copper sulphate. If used in sufficient quantities this prevents germination of the spores. It does not affect the potato plant.

Puff balls (*Lycoperdon*) are basidiomycetes with small, club-shaped fruiting bodies in which the spores are completely enclosed as they ripen. The young fruiting bodies are white and they are edible. Older specimens turn brown. *Calavatia ex-*

Fungi and Lichens 25

to toadstools, except that they have no stalk; the cap of the fruiting body grows directly out of the tree in which the mycelium is growing.

Toadstools can be found growing almost everywhere. Many grow in fields, and probably the best-known species are those of the genus AGARICUS, which includes the tasty field mushroom. Many other kinds can also be eaten, *but some are poisonous, and you must take great care to identify all toadstools correctly before eating them.* If there is one you are at all doubtful about, throw it away.

There are an enormous number of woodland toadstools. Some of these can only be found in certain kinds of woods. This is because they form symbiotic relationships with particular types of tree. The mycelium of the fungus becomes entangled with the roots of the tree to form a structure called a mycorrhiza. Both the fungus and the tree benefit from this relationship, especially in places where the soil is poor. The fly agaric (*see* AMANITA) forms mycorrhizas and is generally found in birchwoods.

Lichens

LICHENS are not single plants; each one is a symbiotic association of an alga and a fungus. The alga is green and makes its own food, some of which is used by the fungus. The alga benefits by getting protection from bright light and dry conditions. Lichens mostly contain single-celled green algae, such as *Pleurococcus*, or filamentous blue-green algae, such as *Nostoc*. The fungi involved are usually ASCOMYCETES.

Many different lichens occur. They may have a leafy or shrubby appearance, or they may form crusts on rocks. Some even grow in the surface layers of rocks. They take the minerals they need from the rainwater that flows over them. Lichens can withstand both extreme cold and heat, and are therefore among the first plant colonizers of regions where harsh conditions prevail. They help to break down the surface of the rocks on which they live, thus starting the process of soil formation.

Lichens can reproduce asexually by forming a powdery mass of structures that contain both the alga and the fungus. Sexual reproduction only involves the production of fungal spores, and a new lichen is formed only if the spores germinate near a suitable algal partner.

Above: Lichens are often found on heathland, where only small, hardy plants such as mosses can survive. The trumpet-shaped fruiting bodies of this lichen produce only fungal spores. A new lichen plant is formed when the spores germinate in the presence of a suitable alga.
Right: Lichens may also be found on cliffs and rocks, where no other plants can grow.

---

cipuliforme is a similar fungus related to the GIANT PUFF BALL.

S **Saprophyte** is an organism that obtains its food as dissolved chemicals from decaying plant or animal tissue. All fungi are either saprophytes or PARASITES.
Stinkhorns are an order of basidiomycetes related to the PUFF BALLS. The spores of the stinkhorn (*Phallus impudicus*) are produced on the end of a short stalk inside the fruiting body. When they are ripe the stalk grows rapidly upwards, forcing its way through the outer covering. The spore mass gives off an unpleasant smell. This attracts flies,

Young shaggy ink caps

which swiftly disperse the spores.
Stipe is the stalk of a toadstool.
Symbiosis is an association between 2 living organisms that harms neither of them and may benefit one or both of them.

T **Toadstools** are the umbrella-shaped fruiting bodies of certain basidiomycetes. The name is commonly used to mean all those except the edible members of the genus AGARICUS, such as the field MUSHROOM.
Truffles (*Tuber*) are a genus

Stinkhorn

of ascomycetes, related to MORELS. They are difficult to find, but excellent to eat.

V **Veil** is the thin membrane that completely covers the young fruiting bodies of the genus AMANITA.

Y **Yeasts** include several types of single-celled ascomycetes, fungi that reproduce by budding. Many yeasts are capable of fermenting sugar to produce alcohol. The yeasts used in baking, brewing and wine making are *Saccharomyces cerevisiae*.

Mosses and Liverworts

Mosses and liverworts are two related groups of mostly small, simple plants. They are great colonizers, because their tiny spores can be carried long distances to new land areas, where they germinate and produce new plants.

Mosses and liverworts are simple, green plants that have no true roots. Instead they are attached to the ground by tiny root-like threads called rhizoids. They live on land and therefore have an advantage over the algae. But their environment must still be moist, because they have no means of preventing their cells from drying out. A moist atmosphere is thus essential for the growth of mosses; it is also necessary for reproduction and for taking in oxygen. Dry conditions kill liverworts and many mosses. However, some mosses can survive even when water is scarce. They shrivel up and appear to be dead. When they are moistened again, they swell up and continue to grow.

Liverworts

The simplest liverworts have no stems or leaves. They have flat plant bodies that spread over the ground. Such plant bodies are called thalli (*see* THALLUS), and liverworts that have this kind of structure are called thalloid liverworts. PELLIA and MARCHANTIA are typical examples of thalloid liverworts.

A more advanced group are called leafy liverworts. These have distinct stems and thin, filmy leaves. However, their stems do not contain any water-conducting cells. The shape of the delicate leaves and the way in which they are arranged on the stem varies considerably. There are many species – over 90 per cent of all the liverworts are leafy liverworts. Examples include LOPHOCOLEA and CALYPOGEIA.

Mosses

Mosses are familiar plants that can be found growing in almost every environment. They are mostly small, low-growing plants with stems and leaves that form mats or small cushions. They only grow to a few centimetres high, but some species spread over a wide area. *Polytrichum commune* is one of the largest European mosses, and may have stems 20 centimetres long. Species of *Dawsonia* in Australia may reach 70 centimetres. The largest British moss is *Fontinalis antipyretica.* It is common in freshwater streams and ponds, where it grows submerged under the water. It grows to a length of about 100 centimetres.

Many mosses, particularly those that can withstand dry conditions, live in places that are unsuitable for higher plants. Together with lichens, they can be found in the Arctic tundra, on rocky mountain tops, on walls, and on the bark of trees. Their ability to live in such inhospitable conditions makes them good pioneering plants. When a new island is formed, mosses and lichens are the first plants to colonize it. For example, in 1963, volcanic action caused

Right: *Polytrichum* is a genus of moss which grows on moorlands. At certain times of the year these mosses produce large numbers of orange-brown capsules, which contain the spores.

Below: Mosses can grow in places that other plants find inhospitable. These mosses are growing on Mount Kenya at 3,500 metres above sea level.

Reference

A Annulus (of a moss) is a ring of large cells round the top of a moss capsule. When the capsule is ripe, the cells of the annulus break and the top of the capsule falls off. The spores can then be released.
Archegonium. This is the female sex organ of a moss, liverwort or fern. It consists of a swollen base, or venter, and a long, hollow neck. The venter contains the female sex cell (oosphere).

Archegonium

B Bog moss, is the popular name for SPHAGNUM.
Bryophytes is the scientific name for mosses and liverworts. They make up the division Bryophyta of the plant kingdom.
Bryum is a genus of mosses. *B. capillare* is a common moss on walls and roofs, where it forms compact green cushions. *B. argenteum* also grows on walls and roofs, and in the cracks between paving stones. It is a dark green moss with a silvery sheen. This species has even been found in the Arizona desert. *B. pseudotriquetrum* grows near mountain streams.

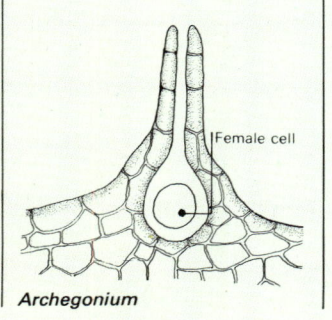

C Calypogeia is a genus of leafy liverworts. *C. bicuspidata* grows in peat bogs, on rotting timber, and on wet soil. *C. fissa* grows in peat bogs, on wet sandy soil, and on sandstone rocks. *C.*

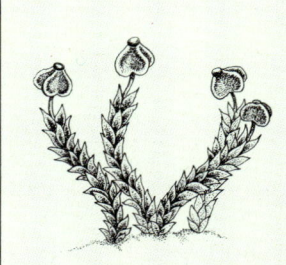

Andreaea rupestris (moss)

meylanii grows on peaty and sandy soils, and on sandstone rocks.
Calyptra is the sheath that completely surrounds the capsule of a moss or liverwort as it develops. It is formed by the growth of the neck of the ARCHEGONIUM.
Capsule, see SPOROGONIUM.
Columella is the central column in a moss capsule. No spores are produced in this region of the capsule.

E Elaters are long, springy cells in the mature capsule of a liverwort. When the capsule opens, the ela-

Mosses and Liverworts

Below: *Pellia epiphylla* is a thalloid liverwort found in moist, shady places. Its round, black capsules are produced in early spring.

Above: *Marchantia polymorpha* is a large thalloid liverwort found in marshy places.

Below: *Riccardia pinguis* is a small thalloid liverwort commonly found in wet places. Its lobes have no midribs.

Above: *Calypogeia meylanii* is a leafy liverwort that grows on peaty and sandy soils and on sandstone rocks.

Below: *Lophocolea cuspidata* is a leafy liverwort that grows on bark in damp woods. Its leaves have 2 large points at their tips.

---

ters help to flick the spores out.

Elaterophore. This is a mass of elaters attached to the inside of the capsule. When the capsule opens, some spores are trapped in the elaterophore and are released at a later time.

F **Fontinalis** is a genus of mosses. *F. antipyretica* is the largest of all the British mosses. It grows submerged underwater, attached to stones in slow-moving streams and rivers.

Funaria is a genus of mosses. *F. hygrometrica* is a common moss that forms patches in fields and on heaths. Its orange-brown capsules hang downwards on the ends of their stalks.

G **Gametophyte** is the generation during the life cycle of a plant that produces sex cells (gametes). The gametophytes of mosses and liverworts are the adult plants. The gametophyte of a fern is the PROTHALLUS (see page 95). Gymnosperms and flowering plants have separate male and female gametophytes. The male gametophyte is the pollen grain, and the female is found within the ovule.

H **Hepaticae** is the scientific name for the liverworts; a class of the division Bryophyta.

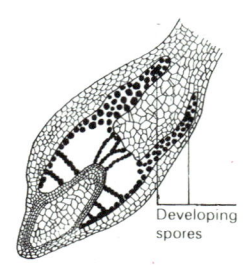

Hypnum cupressiforme is a species of moss of which there are several varieties. Some grow on tree trunks, where they form silky tufts. One variety is found on chalk grassland; it has a rich green colour that may be tinged with yellow or bronze.

I **Involucre** is the outer protective covering of a moss or liverwort SPOROGONIUM. In thalloid liverworts it is formed from two flaps of the THALLUS, above and below the sporogonium. In leafy liverworts and mosses it is formed from leaves around the sporogonium.

L **Lophocolea** is a genus of leafy liverworts. *L. bidentata* is a common liverwort found in grassy places, such as lawns. *L. cuspidata* is found on the bark of trees.

M **Marchantia** is a genus of thalloid liverworts. *M. polymorpha* has a large, spreading THALLUS. It is common in marshy places, the banks of streams, in gardens and greenhouses.

Moss capsule — Developing spores

the island of Surtsey to emerge from the sea near Iceland. Within a few months spores blown from Iceland had landed on the bare rock, and the island was soon colonized by lichens and mosses. Their rhizoids helped to break down the surface of the rock. The powdered rock, together with the remains of dead mosses, began to form pockets of soil. Soon the first flowering plants were growing on the island.

However, the greatest number of mosses occur in damp places, and they grow best where there is little competition from higher plants. For example, the peat bogs are too acid for most plants. Thus the common plants in peat bogs are mosses that can tolerate this acidity. Large hummocks of *Sphagnum papillosum* form here, building up gradually over several years. Eventually the hummocks become so raised that other plants can grow on them. But generally the hummocks break up and the process begins again.

Mosses occur in many other damp places, such as woods and the banks of streams. Many of them will only grow on one type of soil, and it is possible to say whether the soil is acid (for example peat and sand), alkaline (chalk) or rich in nitrogen or phosphorus by identifying the mosses that grow on it.

How mosses and liverworts reproduce

The most important form of reproduction in the mosses and liverworts is sexual reproduction. In fact only the liverworts have any kind of asexual reproduction. *Marchantia* can produce small cup-shaped structures called gemmae on its leaves. When these fall off they can grow into new plants.

The sexual reproduction of mosses and liverworts is more complicated than that found in most algae. They have a method of increasing the number of new plants they produce. Large numbers are important because the young plants are unprotected, and many of them do not survive.

Mosses and liverworts have two generations. One generation produces gametes (sex cells). A fertilized female gamete becomes the second generation plant, which produces a mass of tiny spores. When these germinate, they grow into new gamete-producing plants. This process is

Below: *Mnium hornum* is a common woodland moss that forms large, dull green turfs on wood and peat. In spring the new shoots are a contrasting light green.

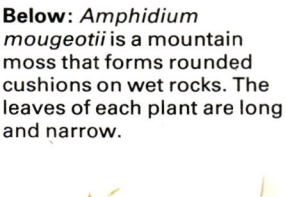

Below: *Bryum capillare* is a common moss on roofs and the tops of walls. Its spore capsules are green when young, but turn brown as they ripen.

Below: *Amphidium mougeotii* is a mountain moss that forms rounded cushions on wet rocks. The leaves of each plant are long and narrow.

Above: *Hypnum cupressiforme* var. *resupinatum* grows on trees, where it forms loose, silky tufts. This is one of several varieties of this moss.

Above: *Sphagnum palustre* is a moss found in the drier, less acid parts of bogs, where it forms pale green mats. It has round spore capsules with circular lids.

Mnium is a genus of mosses. *M. hornum* is one of the most common mosses in woodlands, where it is often found growing on wood or peat. *M. punctatum* is a woodland moss found in shady places near streams. *M. undulatum* is light green moss that grows in shady places. It has upright stems that have a palm-like appearance.
Musci is the scientific name for the mosses; a class of the division Bryophyta.

O **Oosphere**, see ARCHEGONIUM.

Operculum is the cap of a moss capsule. When the capsule is ripe the ANNULUS breaks and the operculum falls off.

Leucobryum glaucum (moss)

P **Paraphyses** are many-celled hairs intermingled with the male and female sex organs (antheridia and archegonia) of a moss. They probably help to keep the sex organs moist.
Pellia is a genus of the thalloid liverworts. *P. epiphylla* grows on the banks of shady streams. *P. fabroniana* grows on wet limestone rocks or on chalky soils.
Peristome teeth are long pointed structures at the top of a moss capsule. They are exposed when the OPERCULUM falls off. They are arranged like the spokes of a wheel and in wet conditions they prevent spores from being released. In dry conditions, the teeth move farther apart, allowing spores to pass through the gaps. Thus spores are only shed in dry conditions, when there is a likelihood of air currents spreading them over a wide area.
Polytrichum is a genus of mosses. *P. commune* is the largest British land moss. It is common on wet, peaty moors. *P. formosum* also grows on moors, but is also found in woods and banks on acid soil. *P. piliferum* forms 'turfs' on sand dunes.
Protonema. This is the thread-like plant that is formed when a moss germi-

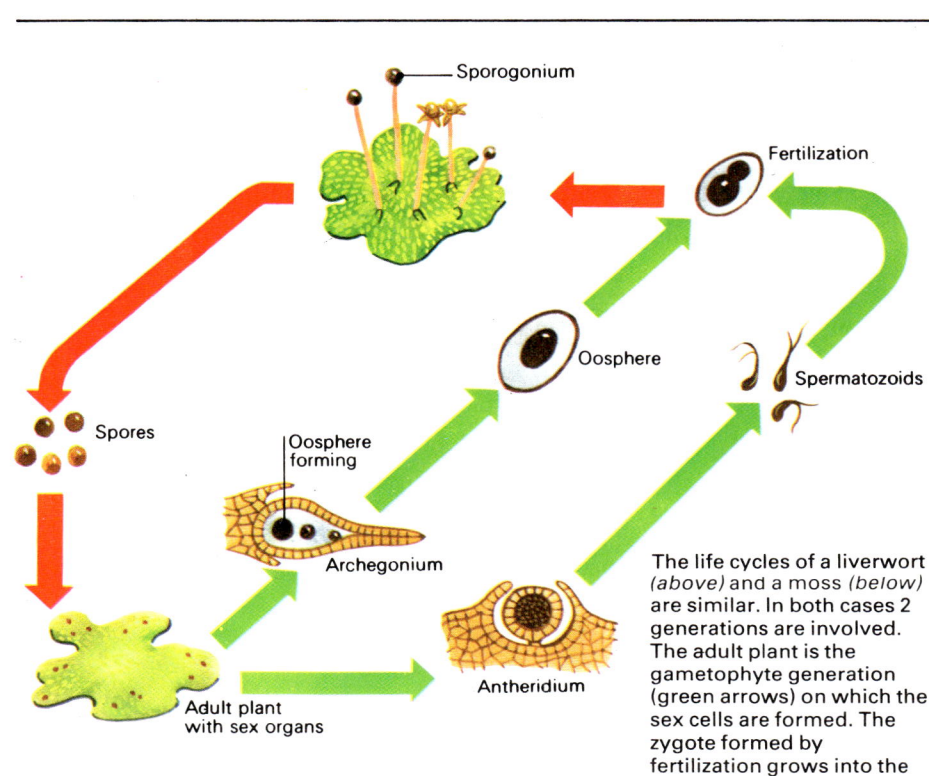

Mosses and Liverworts

The reproduction of a moss is very similar. The adult plant is the gametophyte, but in this case both male and female sex organs grow at the top of the stem. Again, a sporogonium is produced after fertilization, but its structure is more complicated. Mosses also add a further stage to their reproduction. Each spore can grow into a thread-like plant — rather like a filamentous alga — called a protonema. Each protonema produces several buds, which eventually grow into adult moss plants. Thus, by adding the protonema stage, mosses are again able to increase the number of possible new plants.

Alternation of generations is thus an efficient way of producing large numbers of new plants. However, in the sexual reproduction of the mosses and liverworts there is one great disadvantage. The adult plants are gametophytes (gamete-producing plants), and the male gametes (sex cells) need water in which to swim. Therefore, the adult plant must be wet before reproduction can occur. Higher plants have solved this problem, and therefore do not have to live in wet conditions.

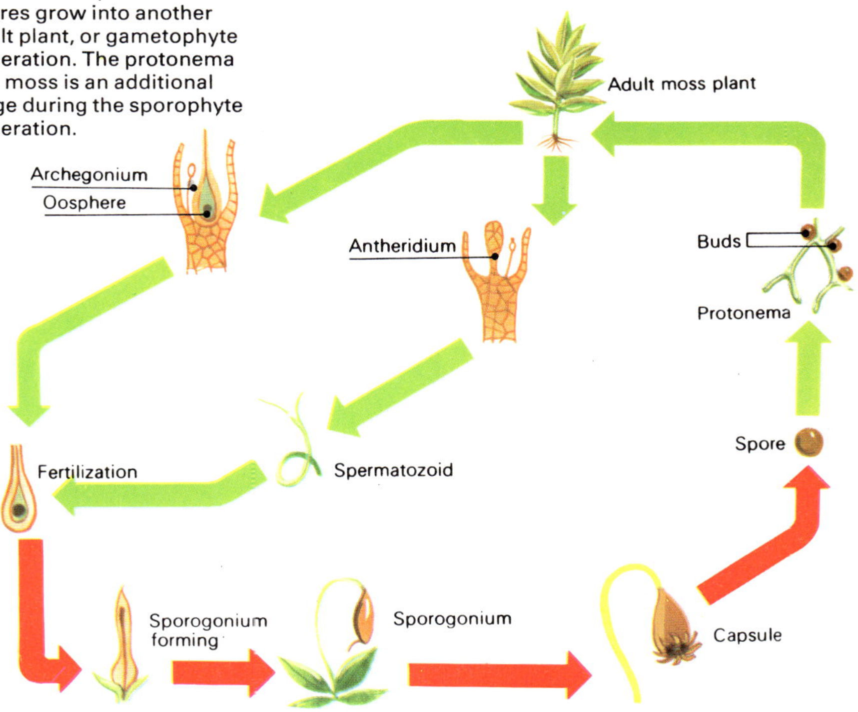

The life cycles of a liverwort *(above)* and a moss *(below)* are similar. In both cases 2 generations are involved. The adult plant is the gametophyte generation (green arrows) on which the sex cells are formed. The zygote formed by fertilization grows into the sporophyte generation (red arrows). This consists of a sporogonium, with its capsule and spores. The spores grow into another adult plant, or gametophyte generation. The protonema of a moss is an additional stage during the sporophyte generation.

called alternation of generations. The gamete-producing generation is called the GAMETOPHYTE, and the spore-producing generation is called the SPOROPHYTE.

The adult plant of a liverwort is the gametophyte generation. On the upper surface of its THALLUS it grows male sex organs (antheridia), which produce male sex cells (SPERMATOZOIDS). Round the edge of the thallus the plant grows female sex organs (ARCHEGONIA), each of which contains a single female sex cell (oosphere). When the sex organs are fully developed, the spermatozoids swim over the wet surface of the thallus, and one spermatozoid fertilizes each oosphere. The fertilized oosphere immediately begins to divide and becomes the second generation — the sporophyte.

The sporophyte generation consists of a capsule on a long stalk. This is called the SPOROGONIUM and it remains attached to the adult liverwort plant. Inside the capsule, meiosis occurs (*see page 11*) and spores are formed. The capsule eventually breaks open, scattering the spores. Each spore is capable of growing into a new liverwort plant and the cycle begins again.

---

nates. It produces several buds, each of which may grow into an adult plant.

R **Riccardia** is a genus of thalloid liverworts. *R. pinguis* is one of the simplest liverworts; it grows in many wet places.

S **Sphagnum** is a genus of mosses, often referred to as bog mosses. They grow in dense masses, and their lower parts are continuously decaying slowly to form peat. There are several species, growing in varying degrees of wetness and acidity.
Spermatozoid is a single male sex cell with flagella, which it uses for swimming.
Spores are single- or many-celled structures formed during the reproductive processes of many plants. They are usually microscopic and are produced in large numbers.
Spore sac is the space inside the moss capsule that contains the spores.
Sporogonium is the structure that develops from a fertilized female sex cell of a moss or liverwort. It is the SPOROPHYTE generation and consists of a spore-containing capsule supported on a stalk, or seta. It is attached to the adult plant (GAMETOPHYTE) by a mass of cells called the foot.
Sporophyte. This is the generation during the life cycle of a plant that produces spores. The sporophyte of a moss or liverwort is the SPOROGONIUM. The sporophytes of ferns, gymnosperms and flowering plants are the adult plants. Gymnosperms and flowering plants produce two kinds of spore. Microspores are pollen grains. Megaspores are single cells that remain inside the ovules.

T **Thallus** is a simple plant body that is not divided into root, stem and leaves.

Lunularia cruciata (liverwort)

Apple moss with capsules

Ferns

Ferns, which may be as small as mosses or as large as trees, were common during the Carboniferous period of the Earth's history. Their remains form a large part of the coal seams which were formed at that time.

Ferns, clubmosses, horsetails, quillworts and psilotes have two main things in common. Their adult plants produce spores, and their stems and leaves contain water-conducting cells. This gives them a great advantage over the mosses and liverworts. They do not have to live in wet conditions, and the adult plants can grow taller. Some of the clubmosses that existed during the Carboniferous period were large tree-like plants, and some modern tropical tree ferns can grow up to 25 metres high.

The first land plants that we know of were the psilophytes (*see page 4*), which became extinct about 370 million years ago during the Devonian period. Two modern plants, PSILOTUM and *Tmesipteris*, resemble them. These very simple plants are called psilotes, and it is possible that they are descended from the psilophytes, although we have no fossil evidence for this.

During the Carboniferous period there were a large number of lycophytes (clubmosses and quillworts). Today only five types exist. These include the clubmosses LYCOPODIUM and SELAGINELLA. Unlike some of their ancestors, such as the large tree-like *Lepidodendron* (*see page 4*), modern club mosses are fairly small, creeping plants. The quillworts, which all belong to the genus ISOETES, are also descended from the lycophytes. These plants do not live on land. They have returned to the water and live permanently submerged. The horsetails are distantly related to the clubmosses and quillworts. In the Carboniferous period large horsetails existed, such as *Calamites,* but today species of EQUISETUM, the only genus that remains, are relatively small plants.

The ferns are a much larger group. There are about 10,000 species distributed all over the world. Most ferns are small plants, and some water ferns are less than one centimetre across. Only the tree ferns grow more than two metres high. Tree ferns and many other types are only found in tropical and sub-tropical rain forests. In fact nearly 75 per cent of all the ferns live in these conditions. Only a few grow in cool and dry climates. In the tropical rain forests, smaller ferns are most often found living in the branches of trees. Here they receive more light than they would on the ground, which is often too swampy to support them. In cooler regions, ferns grow in the soil and among rocks. Most of them are adapted to living in damp and dimly-lit places, but some thrive in dry, sunny habitats and colonize open spaces.

Below: The royal fern (*Osmunda regalis*) is the largest British fern. It grows in wet places, such as the banks of ponds and streams.

Reference

A **Adder's tongue,** see OPHIOGLOSSUM.
Adiantum is a genus of ferns that grow in fairly dry regions. The maidenhair fern (*A. capillis-veris*) grows on sheltered limestone cliffs near the sea. Its delicate fronds have wedge-shaped leaflets.
Arthrophytes is the scientific name for the horsetails (*see* EQUISETUM): a subdivision of the division Pteridophyta.

Asplenium is a genus of ferns that grows on limestone walls or cliffs called spleenworts. Fronds vary according to species.

Ceterach officinarum

B **Botrychium** is a genus of 35 species of ferns found all over the world. *B. lunaria* (moonwort) is a common British fern that grows on rocky ledges and in grasslands. Each plant has a single frond that divides to form a fan-shaped, leafy part and a spherical spore-bearing part.
Bracken, see PTERIDIUM.

C **Clubmosses,** see LYCOPODIUM, SELAGINELLA.

D **Dryopteris** is a genus of typical ferns with long fronds divided into 20-35 main lobes. *D. filix-mas* (male fern), which grows in woodlands, is the commonest species in the British Isles.

E **Equisetum** is the only living genus of horsetails. There are 20 species (10 of which are British), all of which grow in damp places. They have jointed stems, and at each joint there is a ring of small branches. There are no leaves. Spores are produced in cones (*see page 27*) at the tops of stems that are unbranched.

F **Filicophytes** is the scientific name for the ferns; a subdivision of the division Pteridophyta.

H **Hart's tongue,** see PHYLLITIS.
Horsetails, see EQUISETUM.

I **Indusium,** see SORUS.
Isoetes is a genus of water plants known as quillworts. They have a dense tuft of leaves that grow directly from a collection of thick, white roots. They live permanently submerged under the water in lakes and tarns.

Ferns have very small roots and their main underground organ is a creeping stem, or rhizome. This grows horizontally through the ground, putting up new shoots at intervals. In this way ferns can spread over a wide area. The leaves of a young shoot are tightly curled, and they unfold gradually as they grow. Some ferns have very simple, strap-shaped leaves. Others have complicated leaves that are divided many times. These leaves are called fronds, and the smaller divisions are called pinnae.

A few ferns are adapted to special ways of life. For example *Azolla* and *Salvinia* live in water. Their leaves float on the surface and their roots hang down. The upper surface of the fronds is covered with specialized hairs that repel water and ensure that the plant does not sink. Other ferns have methods of overcoming dry conditions. Some species of ASPLENIUM have leaves that shrivel when there is a lack of water, and a number of ferns have fleshy leaves that store water. Ferns that live in the branches of trees have a particular problem in getting all the food they need. Species of *Platycerium*, a type of tropical fern, have overcome this problem. Each plant has special fronds near the base that trap dead plant material. The plant can then absorb what it needs from the resulting humus that forms.

How ferns reproduce

Ferns reproduce asexually when their spreading rhizomes put up new shoots. In swampy tropical rain forests, some ferns produce small plantlets on their fronds. These drop off and grow into new plants. In such conditions this is often the most important form of reproduction.

The sexual reproduction of ferns, like that of the mosses and liverworts, involves the alternation of two generations. In this case the adult plant is the sporophyte (spore-producing plant) and the gametophyte (gamete-producing plant) is very small. In addition, the two plant generations are separate.

Spores are produced in structures called SPORANGIA on the undersides of certain fronds.

Below: *Cyathea smithii* is a tree fern found in New Zealand. Tree ferns are common throughout the tropics.

Below right: Some fern relatives. *Equisetum telmateia* is a horsetail. The stag's horn moss, *Lycopodium clavatum* is a mountain clubmoss. *Psilotum nudum* is a psilote found throughout the tropics and subtropics. *Isoetes lacustris* is a quillwort that grows underwater in lakes.

Equisetum telmateia

Isoetes lacustris

Psilotum nudum

Lycopodium clavatum

L **Lycophytes** is the scientific name for the clubmosses (see LYCOPODIUM, SELAGINELLA) and quillworts (see ISOETES); a subdivision of the division Pteridophyta.
Lycopodium is a genus of clubmosses. There are about 200 species, most of which occur in tropical regions. Some are found in alpine areas and in the Arctic. There are 4 British species. They have long slender stems covered in small leaves.

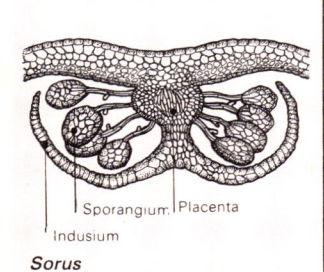

M **Maidenhair fern**, see ADIANTUM.
Marsilea is a genus of water ferns. There are 65 species and they occur in both tropical and temperate regions. The fronds grow from an underwater creeping rhizome, and each frond bears 4 leaflets, rather like a 4-leaf clover.

O **Ophioglossum** is a genus of 45 species of ferns found in almost all the countries of the world. *O. vulgatum* (adder's tongue) is common in grassland in Britain. Like BOTRYCHIUM, to which it is related, it has a single frond. This divides to form an oval leaf and a spore-bearing spike.
Osmunda is a genus of 14 species of ferns found all over the world. *O. regalis* (royal fern) is the largest British fern. It grows in wet places, and the leaflets on the fronds are undivided.

P **Phyllitis** is a genus of ferns related to ASPLENIUM. *P. scolopendrium* (hart's tongue) is the only British fern that has completely undivided, strap-shaped fronds.
Prothallus. A small, green, flat plant, often heart-shaped, that is the gametophyte (see page 27) generation of a fern.
Psilotum is a genus of 2 species of primitive plants. They occur in tropical and sub-tropical regions and grow in the ground among rocks and also in the branches of trees.

Sorus — Sporangium, Placenta, Indusium

Jamaican tree fern

Ferns

Below: The life cycle of a fern involves 2 separate generations. The adult plant is the spore producing plant, or sporophyte (red arrows). A single spore develops into a prothallus, or gametophyte – the plant that produces sex cells (green arrows). After fertilization the zygote develops into a new adult plant.

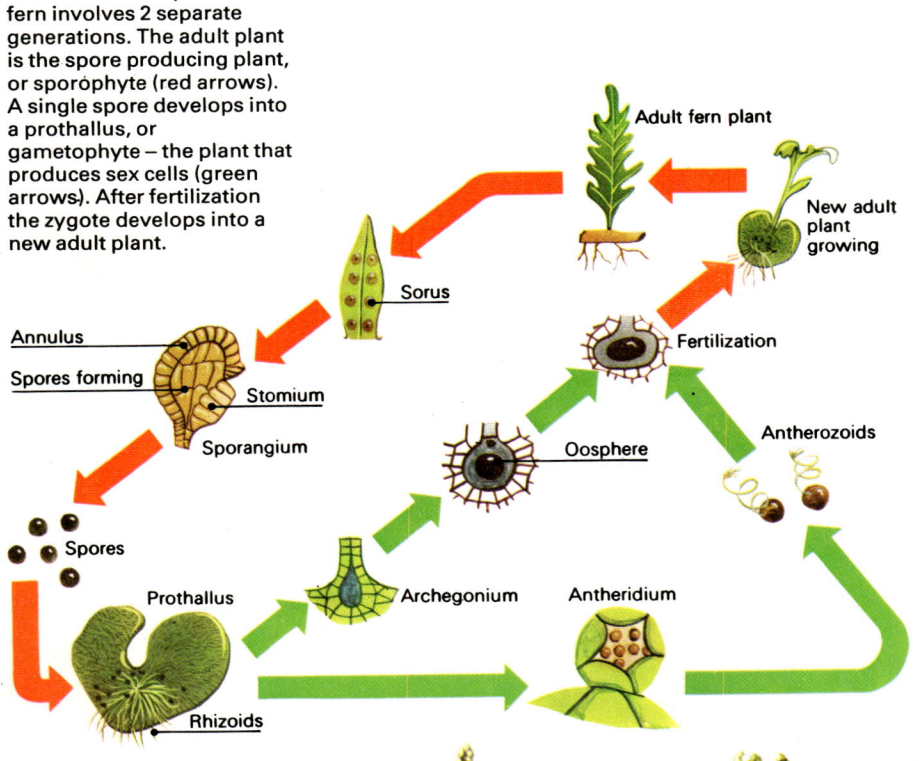

Several sporangia are collected together in a group called a SORUS. You can see these as brown dots on the underneath of a spore-producing frond.

When the sporangia are ripe, the spores are released into the air. They germinate on the ground, and each spore may grow into a tiny heart-shaped plant called a PROTHALLUS. This is the gametophyte generation. Male and female sex organs develop on the upper surface of the prothallus.

The male organs (antheridia) produce male sex cells (antherozoids). These swim to the female organs (archegonia) and fertilize the female sex cells (oospheres). One fertilized oosphere on each prothallus then develops into a new adult plant.

As in the reproduction of the mosses and liverworts, alternation of generations in the fern life cycle ensures that large numbers of new plants are produced. However, in this case the adult plant is the sporophyte, and therefore does not have to live in wet conditions. Only the small gametophyte has to be moist, so that the male sex cells can swim to the female organs.

Below: The hart's tongue (*Phyllitis scolopendrium*) is the only British fern that has undivided, strap-like fronds.

Above: Bracken (*Pteridium aquilinum*) is the most widespread of all ferns, being found in the tropics as well as in temperate regions.

Above: The prickly shield fern (*Polystichum aculeatum*) is a common fern in woods and hedges throughout Britain.

Above: Moonwort (*Botrychium lunaria*) is a fern that grows in grassland and ledges on mountainsides.

Pteridium is a genus of ferns that can successfully compete with flowering plants. This may be due to their very deep systems of rhizomes. *P. aquilinum* (bracken) is the most widespread of all ferns, being found in the tropics, in temperate regions, and even near the Arctic Circle.

Pteridophytes are a group of plants that include the ferns and the 'fern allies' – clubmosses, horsetails, quillworts and psilotes.

Q Quillworts, see ISOETES.

S Selaginella is a genus of more than 700 species of clubmosses. Most of these occur in tropical and sub-tropical regions, but some grow in temperate areas. They are generally found in damp places, such as the floor of rain forests. Some can survive desert conditions. They are similar to LYCOPODIUM in form.

Sorus (plural: sori) is a group of fern sporangia on the underside of a frond. The stalks of the sporangia are attached to a central structure called the placenta. The whole sorus is often covered by a flap called the indusium.

Spleenwort, see ASPLENIUM.

Sporangium. This is the spore-containing structure of a fern. It consists of a capsule on the end of a stalk. A special row of cells runs over the capsule. Some of these cells have thick walls

Epiphytic fern – a fern that lives on a tree

and form the annulus. The remainder have thin walls and form the stomium. When the sporangium is ripe, the cells of the annulus stretch, and the capsule breaks open at the stomium, releasing the spores.

T Tmesipteris is a genus of 2 species of primitive plants found only in Australasia. They grow both in the ground and in the branches of trees. They are related to PSILOTUM, but have larger leaves.

The term gymnosperm comes from two Greek words, meaning 'naked seed'. The most familiar gymnosperms are the conifers, whose seeds are contained in cones. Conifers include some of the world's largest and longest-living trees.

Gymnosperms

Gymnosperms are seed-bearing plants. But, unlike the flowering plants (angiosperms), their seeds are partly exposed. For example, the seeds inside the cone of a pine tree are only protected by scales, which can be lifted off. The seeds of a flowering plant on the other hand, are completely surrounded by the wall of the ovary (*see page 40*). The word gymnosperm means 'naked seed'; angiosperm means 'enclosed seed'.

The best-known gymnosperms are the conifers, which all bear their seeds in cones. But YEWS, CYCADS and Gnetales are also gymnosperms. And the MAIDENHAIR TREE is the only living member of a group of gymnosperms that flourished in the Mesozoic era.

Below: *Cycas media* is a cycad found in Queensland, Australia. There are only 15 species of cycads living.

Above: *Welwitschia* is a strange gymnosperm with long, trailing leaves and cones borne on a short stem.

Yews are evergreen trees found in Europe, Asia and North America. They have long narrow leaves, and for this reason they are often called conifers. However, they do not bear their seeds in cones. Each seed is borne separately and is almost completely enclosed by a fleshy, red, cup-shaped structure that resembles a berry.

Cycads are palm-like trees found only in tropical areas. They have separate male and female plants, and their seeds are produced in large cones in the centre of the female plants.

The Gnetales are a strange group of plants that have some of the features of flowering plants. For example, the water-conducting vessels in their stems are the same as those of flowering plants. However, they bear naked seeds and are therefore generally classed as gymnosperms. The three genera, GNETUM, EPHEDRA and WELWITSCHIA are totally unalike.

The true conifers are the largest group of gymnosperms. They include the PINES, SPRUCES, FIRS, CEDARS, LARCHES and CYPRESSES. They are all evergreen except for the larches and the swamp cypress. They have long, needle-shaped leaves. Each needle is tough and leathery and has a

Reference

C **Cedars** (*Cedrus*) are a genus of 4 species of conifers. The three most important species are the Atlas cedar (*C. atlantica*), which grows in the Atlas mountains of North Africa; the cedar of Lebanon (*C. libani*) from south-western Asia; and the deodar (*C. deodara*) from the western Himalayas.
Cycads (*Cycas*) are primitive gymnosperms found only in the tropics. They have large feathery leaves that arise from an unbranched stem. The lower part of the stem has leaf scars.
Cypresses (*Cupressus*) are a genus of 20 species of trees found in North America, Europe and parts of Asia. They have small, scale-like leaves and round cones.

Cedar of Lebanon

D **Dawn redwood** (*Metasequoia glyptostroboides*) is a deciduous conifer that grows up to 35 metres high. Until 1944 it was only known from fossil remains, and was thought to be extinct. But a small number were found in south-western China, and the tree is now cultivated in gardens as an ornamental.
Douglas fir (*Pseudotsuga menziesii*). A tall conifer (up to 90 metres) found in western America. It has reddish-yellow timber that is used in many kinds of construction, and its tall trunks are used for masts and poles.

E **Ephedra** is a genus of 40 species, most of which are shrubs. They are found in warm deserts in North and South America, and in a belt across Asia from the Mediterranean to China.
Evergreen trees and shrubs are those that have green leaves at all times of the year. Most conifers are evergreen because their leaves do not fall all at once, but over a 3-year period.

F **Firs** (*Abies*) are a genus of tall, pyramid-shaped

Cone of Lebanon cedar

Gymnosperms

Above: There is a wide variety of conifers, which differ in the shape of the tree and its leaves. Those shown are *(left to right)* giant redwood *(Sequoiadendron giganteum)*, cypress *(Cupressus)*, Scots pine *(Pinus sylvestris)*, larch *(Larix)*, and Douglas fir *(Pseudotsuga menziesii)*.

concave surface inside and a convex surface outside. In hot, dry weather the leaf contracts so that it becomes almost cylindrical and this shape helps to reduce the rate of transpiration. As a result conifers can grow in dry places, and also in cold places, where the amount of water in the soil is too low for broad-leaved trees. They can also grow in poor soils that contain few minerals.

Most conifers are found in the Northern Hemisphere. A broad band of coniferous forest stretches round the world just below the tundra zone, and some forests grow as far north as the Arctic Circle. Some conifers are found in hot, dry climates, such as the Mediterranean region and on tropical mountainsides. But only a few occur in the Southern Hemisphere, such as the monkey puzzle tree in the Andes of South America.

Conifers grow quickly and therefore they are useful timber trees. They are called softwoods because their wood is softer and easier to work than broad-leaved trees (hardwoods). Softwoods contain long fibres, and this makes them particularly useful for making paper. They are also used for making plywood, chipboard (chips of wood stuck together with plastic glue), furniture, house-building timber, telegraph poles, mine props, and fence posts.

How a pine tree reproduces

A pine tree, like many other gymnosperms, produces separate male and female reproductive organs on the same tree. The reproductive

---

conifers, with needle-like leaves. There are 35 species. The European silver fir (*A. alba*) is an important timber tree, and the American balsam fir (*A. balsamea*) is a source of turpentine balsam.

G Giant redwood (*Sequoiadendron giganteum*) is the most massive tree in the world, also called giant sequoia, California big tree and Wellingtonia. It is a conifer that grows to over 80 metres high. The largest tree, named General Sherman, is in the Sequoia National Park in California. It is 83 metres tall and has a girth of over 24 metres.

Gnetum is a genus of 40 species of plants that grow in tropical rain forests. They

Maritime pine

are mostly climbing plants, but a few are trees and shrubs. They produce their seeds in cones, but their leaves are identical to those of flowering plants.

H Hemlock (*Tsuga*) is a genus of 10 species of conifers. They are pyramidal in shape and their leaves are needle-like. The western hemlock (*T. heterophylla*) of North America grows to 60 metres high, and its timber is used for paper-making and construction. These trees should not be confused with the herbaceous hemlocks, which are poisonous flowering plants.

J Junipers (*Juniperus*) are a genus of 60 species

Juniper berries

of trees and shrubs found all over the Northern Hemisphere. They are conifers and the male and female cones develop on separate trees. The female cones develop in an unusual way, resembling bluish berries. The 'berries' of the common juniper (*J. communis*) are used for flavouring gin.

L Larches (*Larix*) are a genus of 10 species of deciduous conifers. The European larch (*L. decidua*) is found in mountainous areas and is often planted in gardens.

Gymnosperms

Left: The maidenhair tree (*Ginkgo biloba*) is a 'living fossil'. It is the only living member of a group that from its 2-lobed leaf *(left)*. It is native to China but is rare as a wild tree. It grows well in temperate regions and is often planted in gardens.

fertilize the egg cells. However, only one fertilized egg cell in each ovule develops any further. It begins to divide and grows into an embryo. The cells that surround the egg cell develop into the other parts of the seed. Eventually, each scale in the female cone carries two seeds side by side. Six months after fertilization, in the following spring, the scales of the female cone open again and the seeds are released. Each one has a wing to enable it to be dispersed by the wind.

organs of a pine tree are the cones. Male cones develop from buds in the spring, and several cones may grow from a single bud. Each cone consists of a central rod-like structure surrounded by a number of scales. During the year each scale develops a pollen sac, and by the following spring the pollen is ready to be released. The scales move slightly apart and the pollen sac breaks open. The pollen grains each have two air sacs and they are carried by the wind to the female cones.

The first stage in the development of a female cone also takes about a year. The general structure is the same as that of a male cone. But instead of a pollen sac, each scale produces two female organs called ovules. Pollination occurs in the spring. The scales of the female cone open slightly, allowing the pollen to enter. The ovules each produce a tiny drop of sticky liquid in which the pollen grains are trapped. The scales of the female cone close up again, but fertilization does not occur until the summer of the following year – 18 months later. During this time two egg cells form inside each ovule. Then the sticky liquid dries up, and the pollen grains are released into the ovules.

Special nuclei from the pollen grains then

Right: The life cycle of a pine tree. Each tree produces separate male and female cones. The male cones produce winged pollen grains. The female cones produce 2 ovules on each scale, and each ovule develops 2 archegonia (female sex organs). Fertilization occurs when a nucleus from a pollen grain fuses with the oosphere in an archegonium. Only one archegonium in each ovule develops into an embryo, and the surrounding tissues form the seed coat. When the seeds are fully developed, each scale of the female cone has 2 winged seeds. These are dispersed by the wind, and in favourable conditions an embryo develops into a pine seedling.

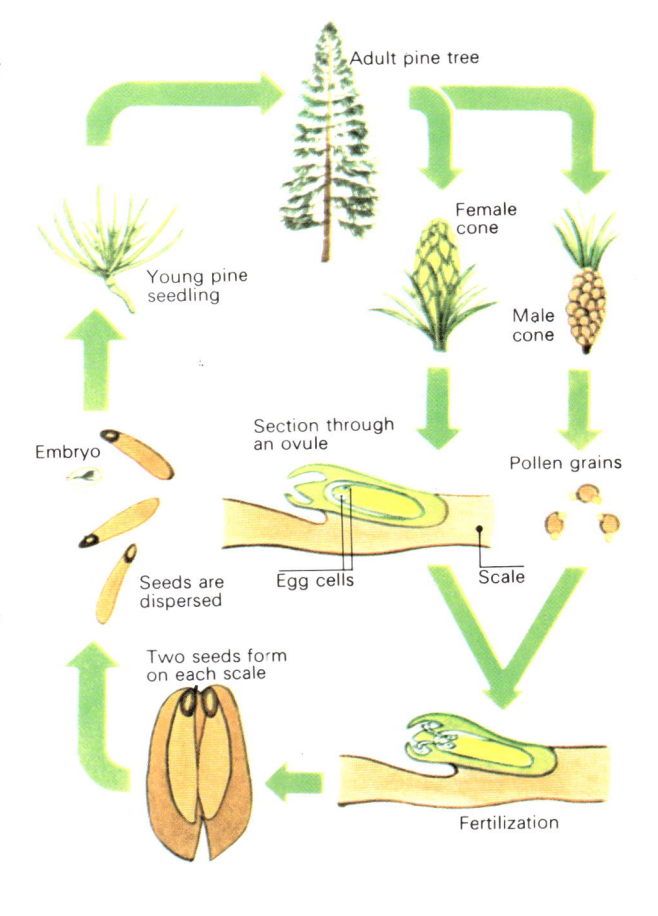

M **Maidenhair tree** (*Ginkgo biloba*) is a very rare tree in the wild, being the only member of the order Ginkgoales, which flourished 200 million years ago. It has distinctive fan-shaped leaves that fall in autumn. The tree is widely cultivated in temperate regions.
Monkey puzzle tree (*Auracaria araucana*) is a strange-looking conifer found in the Chilean Andes of South America. It has small, pointed leathery leaves on branches that are produced in regular tiers.

P **Pines** (*Pinus*) are the largest and most important genus of conifers. There are 80 species found all over the Northern Hemisphere.

Scots pine

The Scots pine (*P. sylvestris*) and the white pine (*P. strobus*) of North America are the most important timber trees.

R **Redwoods** (*Sequoia sempervivens*) are found on the coast of California. Some of them are over 1,800 years old and are the tallest living trees. The tallest specimen is over 111 metres high. *See also* GIANT REDWOOD, DAWN REDWOOD

S **Spruces** (*Picea*) are a genus of 40 species of conifer. They have needle-like leaves that leave peg-like projections on the twigs when they fall.
Swamp cypress (*Taxodium distichum*) is a deciduous conifer found in swampy regions of the USA. It can survive submerged in water for part of the year and grows to a height of 37 metres.

W **Welwitschia bainesii** is the strangest of all the gymnosperms. Its stem is only a few centimetres high, but its long, tapering leaves stretch over the ground. The diameter of the plant may be over a metre. It is found in the coastal desert of South-West Africa.

Y **Yews** (*Taxus*) are a group of evergreen gymnosperms found all over the Northern Hemisphere. The male and female reproductive organs are borne on separate trees. The fruits on the female trees resemble red berries. But the red fleshy part that almost surrounds the seed is actually an outgrowth of the ovule, called an aril.

Flowering Plants

Flowering plants, which dominate our countryside and gardens, form the most varied of all plant groups. Botanists call them angiosperms, the Greek for 'enclosed seeds'. They form about 75 per cent of all land-dwelling plants.

Flowering plants dominate the plant world. Over the last 65 million years they have become so successful that there are now only a few places in which they cannot be found. Their success is due partly to the fact that they have been able to adapt to many different environments. As a result, they are not only a very large group, but also an incredibly varied group. Such very different plants as grasses, trees and cacti are all flowering plants, as well as the more obvious flowers of the countryside.

The flowering plants are divided into two main classes. Monocotyledons (sometimes shortened to monocots) are all those plants that have long thin leaves with veins that run parallel to each other. They get their name from the fact that their seeds contain only one seed leaf, or COTYLEDON. Most monocotyledons in temperate climates are small, non-woody plants. But some tropical monocotyledons, such as PALM trees, are large. Dicotyledons (or dicots) are more varied, but basically their leaves are broader and have a network of veins. Their seeds have two cotyledons.

A flowering plant consists of a root system, stem, leaves, and one or more flowers. The root systems vary considerably. A typical system consists of a single primary root that has branches, or secondary roots. The secondary roots themselves branch repeatedly. The smallest

Below right: Flowering plants with long, thin leaves and 1 seed leaf are called monocotyledons.
Below: Flowering plants range from very simple blooms to intricate arrangements such as in this bird of paradise flower (*Strelitzia regina*).

Orchid

Iris

Coconut palm

Tulip

Reference

A Acacia is a genus of about 500 species of thorny shrubs, mostly found in Australia. They are members of the PEA FAMILY and most species have bright yellow flowers. Their seeds are contained in pods.
Achenes are dry, one-seeded INDEHISCENT FRUITS; e.g. the fruits of the buttercup and dandelion.
Alder (*Alnus glutinosa*). A small British deciduous tree that has dark green leaves and bears catkins. Other alders are found all over the Northern Hemisphere.
Amaryllis family, includes the belladonna lily (*Amaryllis belladonna*), which is a South African plant with bright red flowers. Also in this family are SNOWDROPS, DAFFODILS and the AMERICAN CENTURY PLANT (*see page 49*).
Anemone is a genus of HERBACEOUS plants. A number of species are found all over the world; e.g. the wood anemone in Britain, which produces carpets of pinkish-white flowers in spring.
Annuals are plants that grow, produce seeds, and die within a single season.

Antirrhinum is a genus of plants, commonly called snapdragons. They have dense spikes of red or purple flowers and are found all over the Northern Hemisphere.
Ash (*Fraxinus*) is a genus of about 60 species of deciduous trees found in the cold and temperate regions of the Northern Hemisphere. The common ash (*F. excelsior*) of Europe and Turkey grows to over 30 metres tall.

B Beech (*Fagus*) includes 10 species of deciduous tree that occur throughout the Northern Hemisphere. They are useful timber trees and the most important are the European beech (*F. sylvatica*) and the North Ameri-

Acacia

Flowering ash

Flowering Plants

Above: Wheat belongs to the grass family, which is the largest of all the flowering plant families.
Below: Dictotyledons have broad leaves and 2 seed leaves.

roots are very fine and bear the root hairs that absorb water from the soil. GRASSES have no primary roots. Their root systems are just masses of branching threads. Some plants, such as thistles and dandelions, have long, thick, primary roots called tap roots. These penetrate deep into the soil, seeking out the water that other plants cannot reach.

The stem of a flowering plant is the supporting structure for the leaves and flowers. At its tip is a terminal bud, which is the main growing point of the stem. A simple stem bears leaves at points called nodes. Each leaf is attached to the stem by a leaf stalk, or petiole. Where the petiole joins the stem, an axillary bud forms. This may develop into a side branch. When this happens, the original leaf falls off, leaving a leaf scar, and the branch continues to grow. In woody plants the leaf scar eventually disappears as bark forms and the stem and branch increase in size.

Flowers

When a plant reaches a particular stage in its development it produces one or more flowers. These are shoots specially designed for reproduction. A flower may grow in place of a leaf, or from a terminal or axillary bud.

The main supporting part of a flower is called the receptacle. The remainder of the flower consists of four different sets of organs attached to the receptacle. The outer ring is made up of leaf-like structures called sepals, which are usually green. Inside these are the petals. Insects are attracted to certain colours, and therefore insect-pollinated flowers usually have brightly coloured petals.

The last two sets of organs are the reproductive parts. The male organs (stamens) consist of pollen sacs (anthers) on the ends of long filaments. In the centre of the flower are one or more female organs (carpels). The main part of a carpel is the ovary. This may contain one or more ovules, which contain the egg cells. Projecting from the top of the ovary is a long stalk, called the style. This bears a flat pollen-receiving surface, called the stigma, at the top.

Flowers may be produced singly, as in the case of the tulip. But they are often arranged in a group, or inflorescence. In many inflorescences the individual flowers can clearly be seen. They

Violet | Dog rose | Buttercup | Sunflower | White willow

Oak | Rhododendron

---

can beech (*F. grandifolia*). The popular copper beech is a variety of the European beech.
Bee orchid (*Ophrys apifera*) is a rare orchid whose flower has a broad velvety lip that resembles a bee. It grows on chalkland.
Berries are fruits that have fleshy or pulpy PERICARPS enclosing the seed. They include bananas, gooseberries, marrows, oranges, and dates. *See also* DRUPE.
Biennials are plants that grow, produce seeds, and die within a period of 2 years. During the first year they store up food to be used in the second year, when they produce flowers and seeds. *See also* ANNUALS, PERENNIALS.

Lesser bindweed

Bindweeds are climbing plants that climb by twining their stems anti-clockwise round the stems of other plants. The larger bindweed (*Calystega sepium*) has trumpet-shaped white flowers. The small bindweed (*Convolvulus arvensis*) has cone-shaped pink or white flowers.
Birch (*Betula*) is a genus of about 40 species of deciduous tree found all over the Northern Hemisphere. The bark of these trees is smooth and peels off in layers. It is often silvery-white in colour, like that of the silver birch (*B. pendula*). Other species have black, brown, red, orange or yellowish bark.
Bluebell, see HYACINTH.
Buttercups are a group of flowering plants belonging to the genus *Ranunculus*. This genus also includes the crowfoots and spearworts. Buttercups have cup-shaped, yellow flowers.

C **Calyx** is the outer ring of sepals of a flower. They are usually green, but in some flowers sepals and petals are the same colour.
Campions are members of the PINK FAMILY. They include

Red clover

the white campion (*Silene alba*) and the red campion (*S. dioica*), both of which are common in Britain.
Capsule is a dry, DEHISCENT

Flowering Plants

Horse chestnut stem

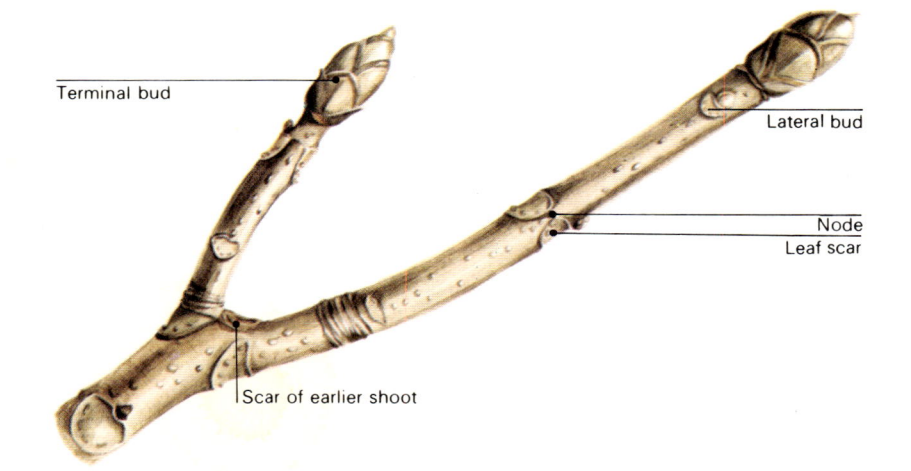

Field geranium

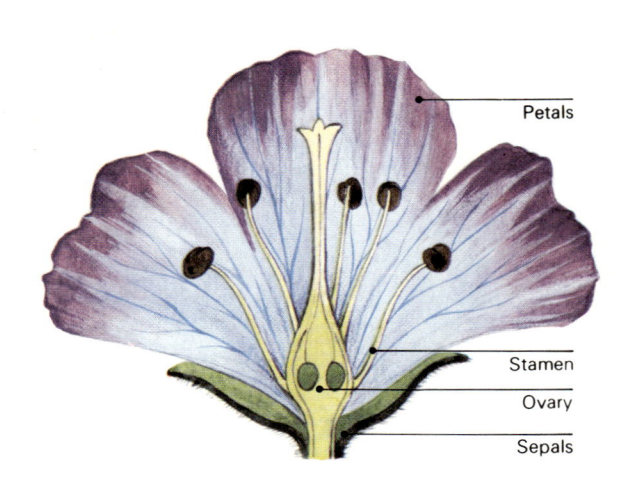

Above: A horse chestnut shoot showing the main parts of a plant stem. In spring the terminal buds open to produce leaves and flowers.

Above right: A section through the flower of a field geranium. The male parts, or stamens, consist of the anthers and filaments. The female part, or carpel, consists of the stigma, style and ovary.

are produced in this way by a branching of the original reproductive shoot. The tall flowering shoot of the FOXGLOVE is an example of the simplest type of inflorescence. However, in some cases the inflorescence becomes so condensed that it looks like a single flower. The 'flower' of a dandelion is in fact made up of a number of tiny individual flowers, or florets.

Pollination

The next stage in the reproduction of a flowering plant involves the transfer of pollen from the anthers of one flower to the stigma of another. This is called cross-pollination. The transfer of pollen from the anthers to the stigma of the same flower is called self-pollination. But this is less desirable. Cross-pollination tends to produce stronger and healthier plants. Self-pollination does occur, but this is usually an accident. Many flowers have evolved ingenious ways of preventing self-pollination.

There are a number of agents for transferring pollen. Pollination by water is rare, as most pollens are damaged by water. In tropical countries some plants are pollinated by birds, such as hummingbirds, and mammals, such as bats, bushbabies and rats, but the vast majority of plants are pollinated by insects or wind.

Wind-pollinated plants produce light, dusty pollen. Large amounts of this pollen are needed to ensure that some of it reaches other plants. Grasses are typical examples of wind-pollinated plants. A grass flower spills out pollen from large anthers on the ends of long, hanging filaments. Some of this pollen is collected by the feathery stigmas of other grass plants. Maize produces two kinds of flower on each plant, but the male and female flowers are well separated. This ensures that the pollen has a greater chance of reaching the female flowers on other nearby plants. Alder and hazel trees, too, have separate male and female flowers, which grow in inflorescences called catkins. WILLOW trees also produce catkins, but in this case the male and female catkins are grown on completely separate trees.

Insect-pollinated plants first have to attract insects to their flowers. Here, the colours of flowers play a large part. Experiments have shown that insects respond particularly to blues, mauves and purples. They see red only as a shade of grey. Thus in temperate climates there are very few naturally occurring pure red flowers. Some insects also respond to varying shades of ultra-violet light, which is invisible to humans. Thus some flowers that seem white to us do not appear white to insects.

In addition to colour, flowers often have particular markings, such as lines and coloured spots. These help the insects to find their way into flowers. The bee orchid has an even more elaborate arrangement. The flowers resemble female bees in appearance, odour and feel and

---

FRUIT that usually contains many seeds. The fruits of poppies, ANTIRRHINUMS, and irises are capsules.

Clematis is a genus of climbing plants that includes old man's beard (*C. vitalba*). This gets its name from the masses of feathery fruits produced by each flower. It is also called traveller's joy.

Clover (*Trifolium*) is a genus of over 300 species of HERBACEOUS plants. They are found all over the Northern Hemisphere and South America. The majority of them have 3 leaves joined at the base. Their flowers are small, arranged in a round head and may be red, white or yellow.

Corolla is the petals of a flower.

Crocus

Cotyledons are the seed leaves that form part of the embryo in a seed.

Cow parsley (*Anthriscus sylvestris*). A tall fern-like plant that bears masses of white flowers in flattened heads. It is a very common plant.

Cowslip (*Primula veris*). A herbaceous plant related to the PRIMROSE. However, its flowers and leaves are smaller than the primrose's.

Crocus is a genus of monocotyledons consisting of about 80 species. The petals and sepals of their flowers are alike.

D **Daffodil** (*Narcissus*) is a genus of about 50 species of monocotyledons found in Europe, Asia, and North Africa. The flowers

Ox-eye daisy

have 6 white or yellow outer segments. Inside these there is a trumpet-shaped tube, which is generally yellow, orange or red.

Daisy (*Bellis*) is a genus of small HERBACEOUS plants found in many parts of the world. *B. perennis* is a common weed on lawns in Britain. The flower head of a daisy is made up of yellow disk florets surrounded by a ring of white ray florets.

Dandelion (*Taraxacum*) is a genus of herbaceous plants related to the daisy. Their flower heads are made up of yellow ray florets.

Flowering Plants

thus attract the male bees, who pollinate the flowers.

Some flowers attract bees, others attract moths, butterflies, beetles, or other insects. An insect attracted to the flower, must then be stimulated so that it performs the right actions. The nectar of a flower is the usual stimulant. It is produced in glands called nectaries at the bases of the petals. In drinking the nectar an insect picks up pollen from the anthers. At the same time it may brush pollen it is carrying from another flower on to the stigma.

Like wind-pollinated flowers, insect-pollinated varieties have various ways of preventing self-pollination, or at least reducing the possibility of its occurrence. For example, in some flowers the stamens and stigmas ripen at different times.

Other plants may produce two or three different types of flower. For example, the PRIMROSE has pin-eyed and thrum-eyed flowers on separate plants. The pin-eyed flowers have stamens well below the prominent stigma. In thrum-eyed flowers the positions are reversed, and the stamens are above the stigma. An insect visiting a pin-eyed flower gathers pollen on the front end of its body. When it visits a thrum-eyed flower, the pollen is brushed on to the stigma, and the insect collects pollen on the rear end of its body. This pollen can then pollinate a pin-eyed flower. The purple LOOSESTRIFE has an even more complicated arrangement of three types of flower. Pollen from each type can be used to pollinate the other two.

Many flowers are shaped so that an insect can only enter in a certain way. These flowers often have elaborate mechanisms for preventing self-pollination. In the violet flower, the four lower petals are arranged as a landing platform for the insect. Inside the flower the pollen-receiving part of the stigma is covered by a flap. A visiting insect automatically pushes open this flap and deposits pollen on to the stigma. The construction of the anthers is also modified so that a kind of pollen-collecting box is formed. The insect is showered with pollen from the box as it pushes into the flower to drink the nectar. This pollen cannot be deposited on the stigma because the flap closes as the insect backs out of the flower.

A few flowers use scent rather than colour to attract the insects in the first place. The LORDS-

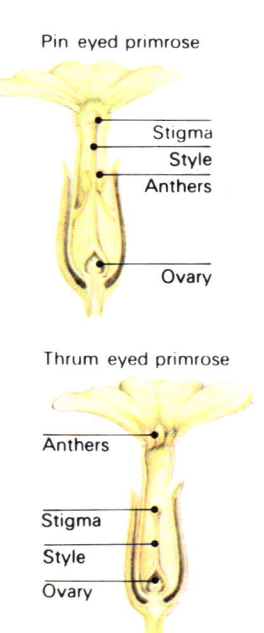

Above: Primroses have 2 kinds of flower in order to prevent self-pollination. The anthers and stigmas are in different positions. Pollen from one kind of flower is transferred to the stigma of the other kind.

Left: Catkins of the silver birch tree shedding pollen into the wind.

Right: The flowers of bee orchids look like female bees. This attracts male bees, which pollinate the flowers.

Deadly nightshade, see NIGHTSHADE FAMILY.
Deadnettle, see NETTLE.
Deciduous tree. A tree that sheds its leaves at a particular time of year, usually the autumn. *See also* EVERGREEN.
Dehiscent fruit. A fruit that opens in an organized manner in order to release its seeds. *See also* INDEHISCENT FRUIT.
Dioecious plant. A species of plant in which male and female flowers are borne on separate individuals. *See also* MONOECIOUS.
Dogwood (*Cornus*) is a genus of about 40 species of deciduous trees, found in northern temperate regions. The European red dogwood (*C. sanguinea*) has leaves that turn blood-red in autumn, and its bark turns red in winter.
Drupe. A fruit in which the outer layers of the PERICARP are fleshy or fibrous. But, unlike a BERRY, the inner layers surrounding the seed are stony. Examples of drupes include plums, cherries, peaches and coconuts. Blackberries and similar fruits are collections of drupes.

Deadly nightshade

E Elder (*Sambucus nigra*) is a European shrub that grows to about 10 metres high. Although the shrub smells unpleasant, its cream-coloured flowers and black fruits can be used to make excellent wine.
Elm (*Ulmus*) is a handsome deciduous tree that can

Elder

grow to over 30 metres tall. There are about 20 species found all over the Northern Hemisphere. However the English elm (*U. procera*), one of the grandest species, is being severely reduced in numbers by Dutch elm disease – a fungal disease carried by beetles.
Epigeal germination. A form of seed germination in which the cotyledons emerge from the seed case and photosynthesize. *See also* HYPOGEAL GERMINATION.
Endospermic seed. A seed in which the endosperm (food store) lies outside the

Flowering Plants

From flower to seed

After a pollen grain has landed on a stigma, it begins to develop a tube. This grows down through the style. Inside the tube are two sperm nuclei and a tube nucleus. When the tube reaches the ovule, fertilization occurs. One sperm nucleus fuses with the ovum, which begins to develop into an embryo. The other sperm nucleus fuses with the two cells next to the ovum, called polar cells. The resulting cell grows into the seed food-store, or endosperm.

Fruits and seeds

A mature seed consists of the embryo and its endosperm surrounded by a seed coat, or testa. The testa is formed from the layers that once surrounded the ovule. The seed is contained in a fruit, which is formed from the ovary wall.

Left: A lords-and-ladies flower head cut away to show the flowers inside the green sheath. Small insects fall into the bottom of the sheath, where they pollinate the female flowers.

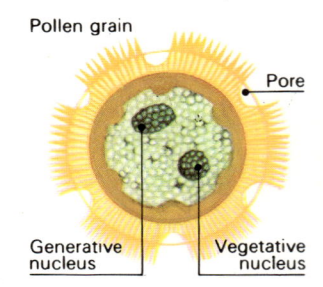

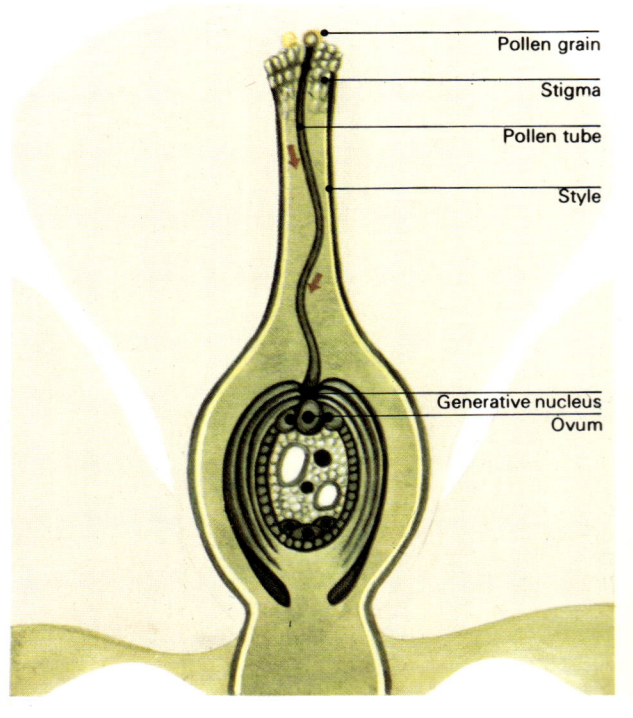

AND-LADIES flowering shoot consists of a spike of flowers surrounded by a green sheath. The flowers are arranged on the spike in two groups – female near the base and male above. Above the flowers is a fringe of hairs and the whole spike is covered in a sheath. At the top of the spike is a club-shaped organ that produces a rotten smell, which attracts insects. The inside of the green sheath is slippery and small insects slide down and become trapped. Then they are held during the night. The downward pointing hairs prevent large insects from entering. If the small insects are carrying pollen from another flowerhead, the female flowers will be pollinated. Then the male flowers ripen and shower the insects with pollen. By next morning the slippery surface has disintegrated, thus allowing the insects to escape carrying the pollen. Sooner or later the process will be repeated.

Right and **above right**: A pollen grain contains a generative nucleus and a vegetative nucleus. When it lands on a stigma the generative nucleus divides into 2 sperm nuclei. The pollen grain then grows a tube, which pushes its way down the style. When it reaches the ovule, the vegetative nucleus disintegrates and one sperm nucleus fuses with the ovum. This then grows into the embryo. The other sperm nucleus fuses with some of the nuclei surrounding the ovum. This then grows into the endosperm (food store) of the seed.

COTYLEDONS. As the embryo grows, the cotyledons absorb the endosperm.
Eucalyptus is a genus of over 500 species of shrubs and trees, found in Australia and Tasmania. Many species grow to over 30 metres high, and the giant gum of Victoria (*E. regnans*) may reach 90 metres. Some species are grown for the oil that is produced in their leaves.
Evergreen is a shrub or tree that bears leaves all year. See also DECIDUOUS.

F Follicle is a dry fruit, formed from a single carpel, that opens by splitting down one side of the fruit. The fruits of monkshood (*Aconitum*) are follicles.

Forget-me-not (*Myosotis*) is a genus of HERBACEOUS plants with small, blue flowers. They are common in Europe, except for the mountain forget-me-not (*M. alpestris*).
Forsythia is a genus of 6 species of shrubs. They have bright yellow flowers that appear in spring before the leaves open.
Foxglove (*Digitalis purpurea*) is a BIENNIAL herbaceous plant that produces a spike of purple flowers. The leaves contain the poisonous drug digitalin, used to treat heart disease.

Fuchsia is a genus of about 100 species of shrubs, found in Central and South America, and New Zealand. The flowers are red, purple or white and the coloured sepals surround a tube formed by the petals.

G Geranium is a genus of about 160 species of herbaceous plants. The flowers are white, pink or blue. Wild geraniums include herb robert (*G. robertianum*) and several kinds of cranesbill. Greenhouse geraniums have all been bred from the genus *Pelargonium*.

Gorse (*Ulex europaeus*) is a tough plant whose leaves are modified into spines. It belongs to the PEA family and has yellow flowers.

Foxgloves

Geraniums

Flowering Plants

Plum
- Edible mesocarp
- Hard endocarp
- Seed

Below: Sections of plum and apple fruits show how they are constructed. The fruit of a plum has 2 layers. The hard endocarp protects the seed. The true fruit of an apple is only the core, which develops from the ovary. The edible part is the swollen receptacle.

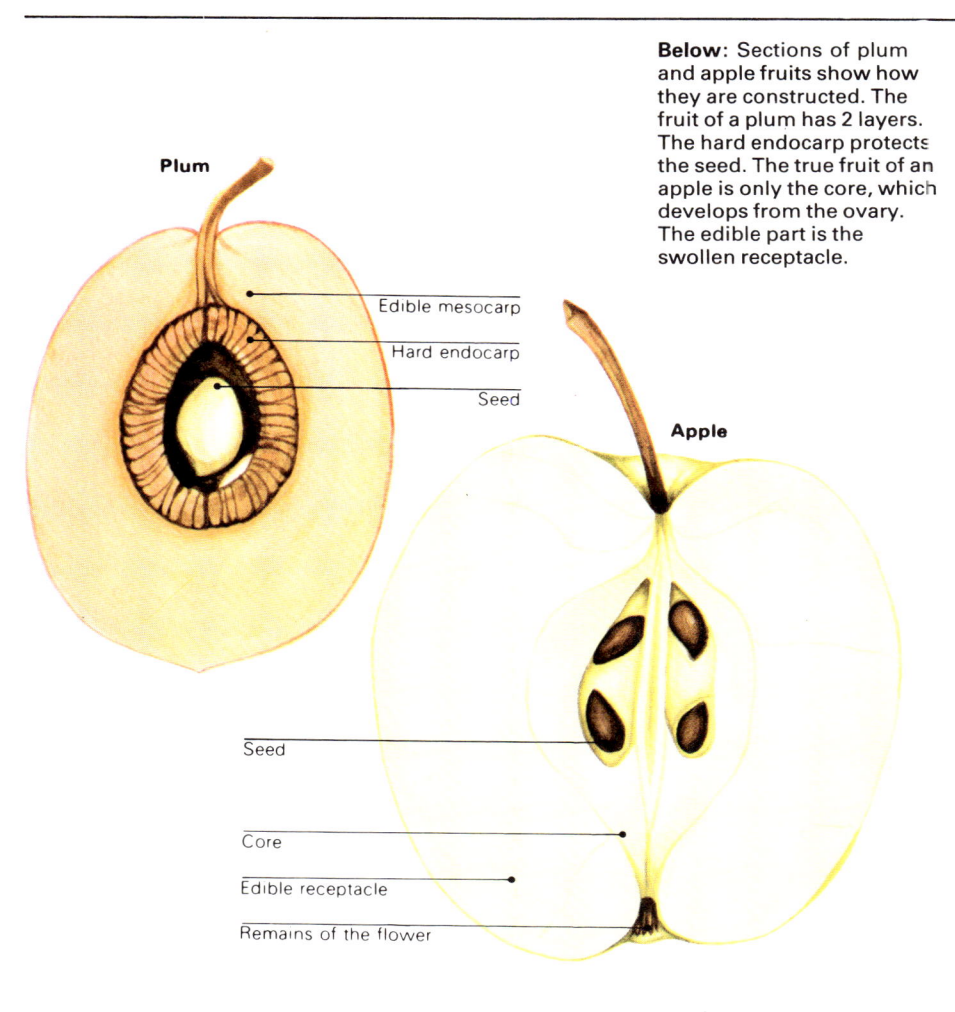

Apple
- Seed
- Core
- Edible receptacle
- Remains of the flower

Sometimes other structures, such as the petals, sepals, or receptacle are involved in the formation of a fruit. Such fruits are described by botanists as false fruits.

There are many different kinds of fruits. Each structure is related to the way in which the seeds inside are dispersed. As in the case of pollination, wind, water and animals all play a part in seed dispersal.

Wind dispersal is very common. The simplest form of wind-dispersed seed is found in some parasites and ORCHIDS. The seeds are small and light, and can be blown like dust. The poppy has a more elaborate mechanism. The seeds are contained in a capsule that sways in the wind. As it moves, the seeds are shaken out of tiny holes.

Some fruits have wings or parachutes. The wings of sycamore and ASH fruits spin like the blades of a helicopter rotor. The seeds are thus carried slowly to the ground. But as they fall the wind may carry them some distance from the tree. These wings have such excellent aerodynamic properties that they were studied by the pioneer aircraft builders in the 1800s. Parachuted fruits include those of the dandelion and old man's beard. The parachutes are made up of tiny hairs, and these fruits can be carried by the wind over long distances.

Dispersal by animals may occur in one of several ways. Sweet, succulent fruits, such as blackberries and plums, may be eaten by birds or mammals. They contain hard, indigestible seeds

Right: Fruits and seeds are dispersed in a number of ways. Dandelion and sycamore fruits are dispersed by the wind. Poppy seeds are shaken out of the holes in the top of the capsule. Laburnum seeds are ejected explosively as the pod twists open. Hazel nuts are hidden away by squirrels. Burdock fruits have hooks that catch on to the fur of animals. Strawberries are eaten by animals and the true fruits (achenes) on the outside of the swollen, red receptacle pass through the animal unharmed.

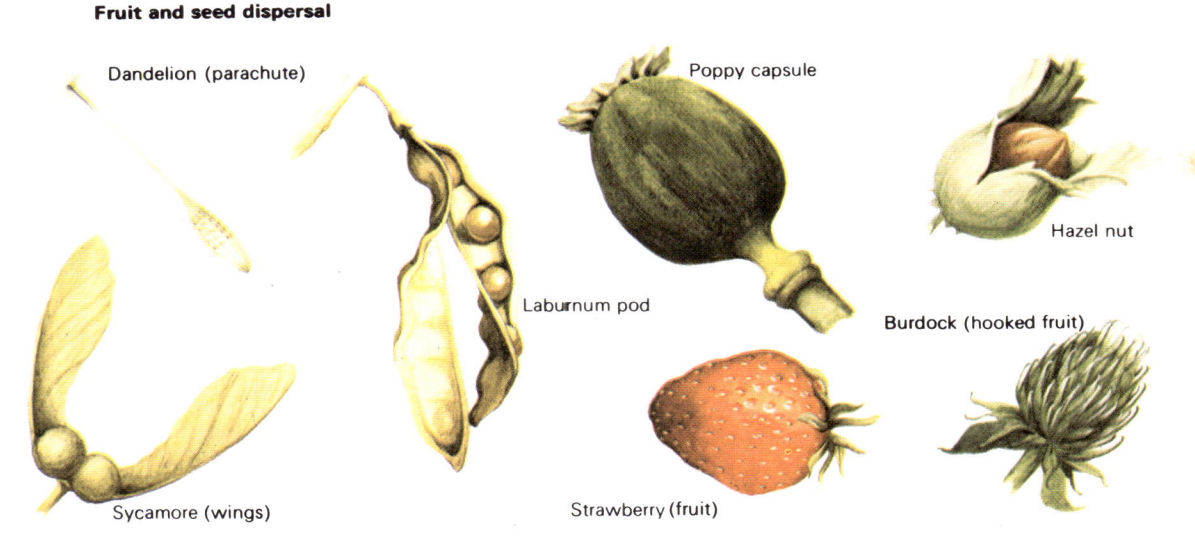

Fruit and seed dispersal
- Dandelion (parachute)
- Sycamore (wings)
- Laburnum pod
- Poppy capsule
- Hazel nut
- Burdock (hooked fruit)
- Strawberry (fruit)

Grasses are a large family of monocotyledons. There are over 10,000 species including bamboos, sugar cane, and cereal crops, such as maize and wheat.

Groundsel are a few species of herbaceous plants belonging to the genus *Senecio*, which also includes the ragworts. They are all related to the daisy and have yellow flower heads.

H Hazel (*Corylus*) is a genus of 15 shrubs and trees found in northern temperate regions. The filbert (*C. maxima*) and the European hazel (*C. avellana*) both produce edible NUTS.

Heartwood is the wood found in the centre of a tree trunk. It has no living cells, and the xylem cells have become blocked, and so are not used for conducting water. It is more resistant to decay than SAPWOOD, and it gives the tree its strength. The pigments found in the heartwoods of ebony, rosewood and walnut make them very attractive for furniture.

Hemlock (*Conium maculatum*) is a very poisonous herbaceous plant related to COW PARSLEY, which it resembles. But it can be distinguished by its unpleasant smell and its smooth, purple-spotted stem. A drug extracted from the leaves is now used in medicine.

Herbaceous plant is a plant without a woody stem.

Honeysuckle

Horse chestnut flower

Holly (*Ilex aquifolium*) is an EVERGREEN shrub with tough, shiny, prickly leaves. It is DIOECIOUS and the familiar red berries develop on the female tree when there is a male tree nearby.

Hollyhock (*Althaea rosea*) is a herbaceous garden plant, originally from Asia. It is a tall plant and bears many red, yellow, or white flowers.

Honeysuckle (*Lonicera*) is a climbing plant with heavily scented flowers that open in the evening. The wild honeysuckle, or woodbine (*L. periclymenum*), has white or

42 Flowering Plants

which pass undamaged through the animals. They may thus be dropped a long way from the parent plant. Hazel NUTS and oak acorns may be taken and stored by squirrels. In this case it is the absent-mindedness of the squirrels that ensures the dispersal of the seeds. They often forget where the nuts are hidden. Some dry fruits have hooks or spines on their surface. These catch on an animal's fur and are carried away.

Explosive mechanisms occur in several plants whose seeds are contained in pods or capsules. The two halves of a pea pod try to twist apart as its fibres dry out. Eventually, the strain bursts the pod, and the seeds are hurled out. Similar explosive mechanisms are found in *Laburnum* and *Geranium*. An unusual mechanism is found in the squirting cucumber. The seeds are forced out by fluid pressure, which builds up as the inner wall of the fruit breaks down.

Few fruits are dispersed by water, as the seeds are usually damaged. However, the fruits of the coconut have a thick, fibrous outer covering. This is waterproof, and the seeds may be carried over thousands of kilometres by ocean currents.

Above: Many animals eat the tasty fruits they can find. The seeds of a blackberry are sufficiently tough to pass through this dormouse without being harmed. This ensures widespread dispersal of seeds.

Left: Old man's beard gets its name from the mass of feathery fruits it produces in the autumn. They are dispersed by the wind.

From seed to plant

After a seed has been dispersed it may begin to grow into a new plant. This is called germination. Most seeds need three things in order to germinate — water, light and warmth. Given these conditions some seeds germinate immediately. But other seeds may remain inactive for some time. This period in which the seed appears to do nothing is called dormancy, which literally means 'sleep'. Many seeds lie dormant during the winter months and germinate in the spring.

Germination begins when water enters the seed, causing it to swell. The embryo then begins to grow. First, it produces a tiny root, called the radicle. This grows down into the soil and helps to anchor the young plant. Next, the embryo produces a small shoot, or plumule. This grows upwards towards the light.

During this time the young plant is using the

---

pale pink flowers, which turn orange-brown after pollination. There are several cultivated species.

Hornbeam (*Carpinus*) is a genus of 21 species of deciduous tree found in northern temperate regions. The Eurasian hornbeam, or yoke elm (*C. betulus*), can grow up to 18 metres high.

Horse chestnut (*Aesculus hippocastanum*) is an ornamental tree thought to have come from Greece, but now found all over Europe and North America. Its white or pink flowers grow in large erect spikes.

Hyacinths are all members of the lily family that grow from bulbs. The wild hyacinth, or bluebell (*Endymion nonscripta*) is found all over Europe. Cultivated hyacinths are all derived from the Lebanese species, *Hyacinthus orientalis*.

Hypogeal germination is a form of seed germination in which the cotyledons remain underground and play no part in photosynthesis. See also EPIGEAL GERMINATION.

Indehiscent fruit is a fruit from which the seeds are not deliberately released. The seeds may germinate within the PERICARP, or they may be released by accidental breakage of the pericarp.

Ivy in flower

Iris is a genus of monocotyledons that includes over 200 species in the Northern Hemisphere. The outer segments of iris flowers are drooping; the inner segments are erect.

Ivy (*Hedera helix*) is a woody, evergreen climbing plant found throughout Europe. Other species are found in Asia and the Canary Islands. Ivy climbs by small roots that attach themselves to stone or bark by a cement-like substance.

Jacaranda is a genus of 500 species of shrubs

Laburnum

and trees from Central and South America.

Judas tree (*Cercis siliquas-*

Flowering Plants

Below: A broad bean seed has its endosperm inside its 2 cotyledons. The cotyledons remain below ground during germination. This type of germination is called hypogeal. The endosperm supplies the developing plant with food until the first leaves appear. These then photosynthesize.

Below: A maize (sweetcorn) seed has a single cotyledon that remains below the ground all the time. The endosperm is not contained within it. The plumule is surrounded by a sheath called the coleoptile. The leaves develop inside this until they force their way through the top.

Below: A castor oil seed has its endosperm outside its cotyledons. But both are pushed above the ground during germination. This type of germination is called epigeal. The endosperm is absorbed by the cotyledons until they grow too large to be held within the seed case.

food reserves contained in the endosperm. In some seeds the endosperm is contained in the seed leaves, or cotyledons. In others the endosperm is separate from the cotyledons. In either case the seed may germinate in one of two ways.

During the germination of the sunflower seed, the cotyledons, which contain the endosperm, are pushed above the soil as the plumule grows. They quickly turn green and begin photosynthesis (*see page 13*). This also occurs when the castor oil seed germinates, although in this case the endosperm is not contained in the cotyledons. When the cotyledons emerge from the seed case, the endosperm is left behind.

In the other type of germination, the cotyledons remain underground. For example, the large cotyledons of the broad bean seed never emerge from the soil. They contain the endo-

Below: A coconut may be carried for many thousands of kilometres by ocean currents before germinating on some tropical shore.

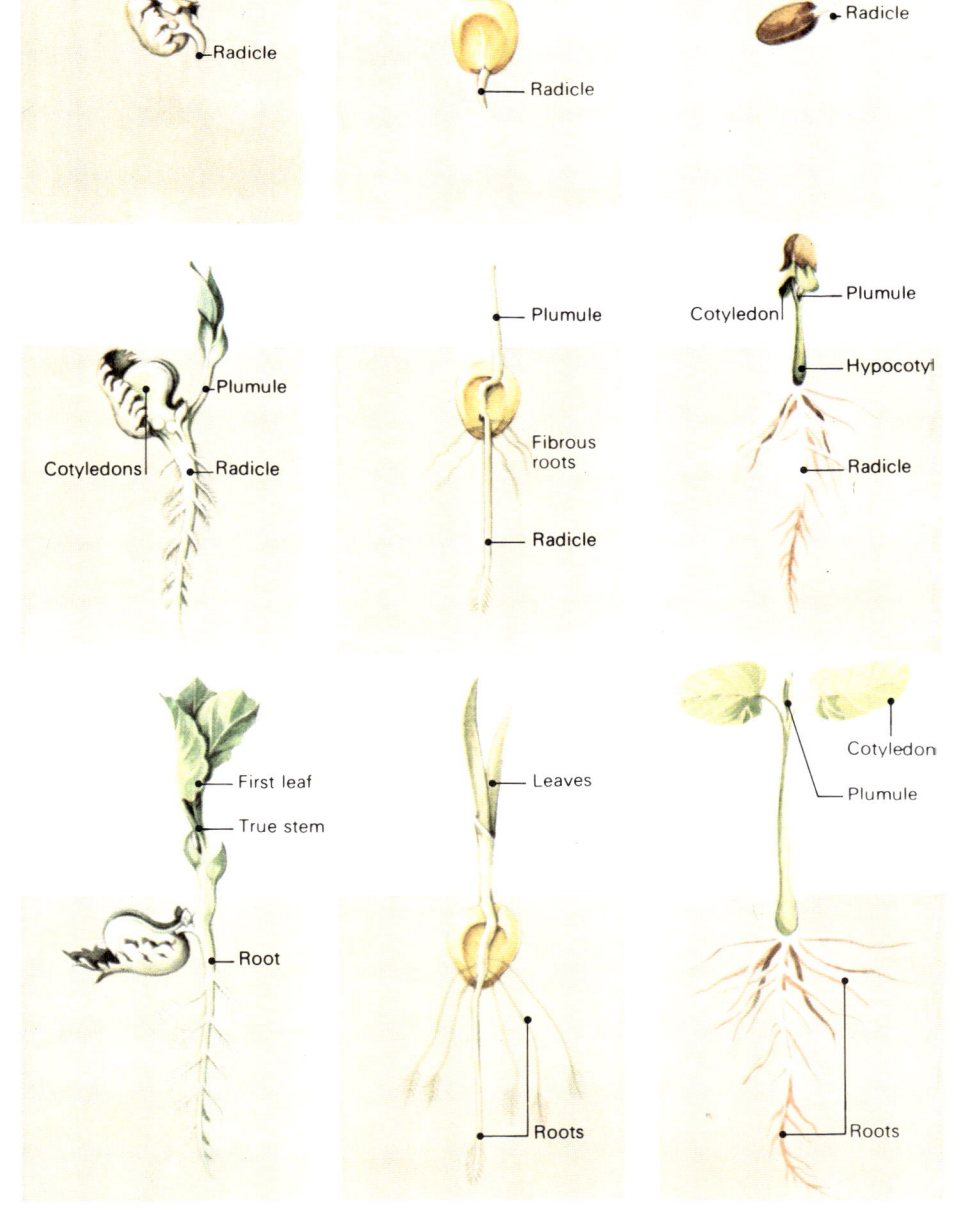

---

trum) is a beautiful deciduous tree found in southern Europe and Asia. It has pink flowers that open before the leaves in the spring. It is so called because Judas Iscariot is supposed to have hanged himself from one.

Laburnum is a genus of 3 small trees found in Europe and Asia. They belong to the PEA FAMILY, and produce seeds in pods.
Laurel family is a family of deciduous and evergreen shrubs including the bay laurel (*Laurus nobilis*), whose leaves are used in cooking. The avocado pear and the sassafras are also in this family. The common laurel (*Prunus laurocerasus*) belongs to the ROSE FAMILY.

Common laurel

Legume is a pod or dry fruit formed from a single carpel, that opens by splitting down both sides. The term legume is often used to describe the type of plant that produces pods. For example, peas, beans, *Laburnum*, clover, and *Acacia* are all legumes.
Lily (*Lilium*) is a genus of about 80 species of monocotyledons found in northern temperate regions. They have large, showy flowers of all colours except blue.
Lily of the valley (*Convallaria majalis*) is a monocotyledon that grows in northern temperate regions. It has a creeping underground rhizome, broad, pointed leaves, and white, bell-like flowers.
Lime (*Tilia*) is a genus of about 30 species of deciduous trees. Their soft, white wood is used for carving.
Loosestrife is a family of 50 species of trees, shrubs and HERBACEOUS plants. It includes the purple loosestrife (*Lythrum salicaria*), which is a herbaceous plant found in Europe. It has 3 different types of flower to ensure cross-pollination. The dye henna is obtained from the leaves of one of this family, *Lawsonia inermis,* which is a shrub found in North Africa and south-west Asia.
Lords-and-ladies (*Arum maculatum*) is also known as

Lilies of the valley

Flowering Plants

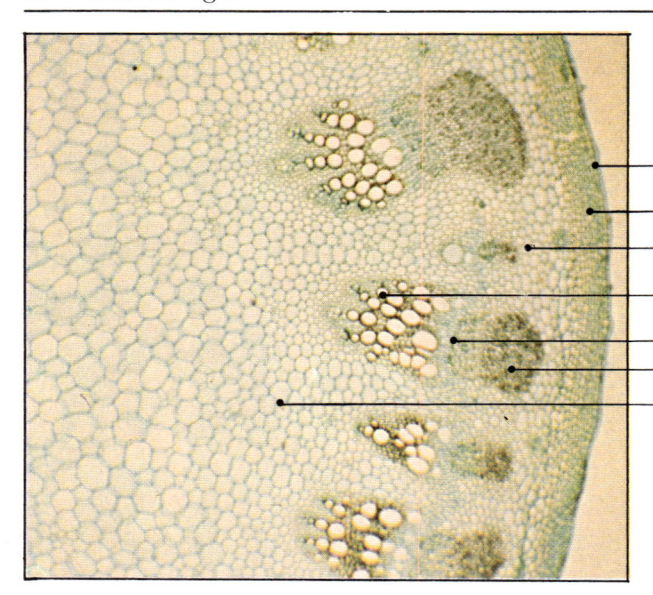

Left: A cross-section through a sunflower stem
Right: A cross-section through a maize stem.

- Epidermis
- Collenchyma
- Parenchyma
- Xylem
- Phloem
- Cambium
- Schlerenchyma fibres
- Parenchyma of pith
- Parenchyma

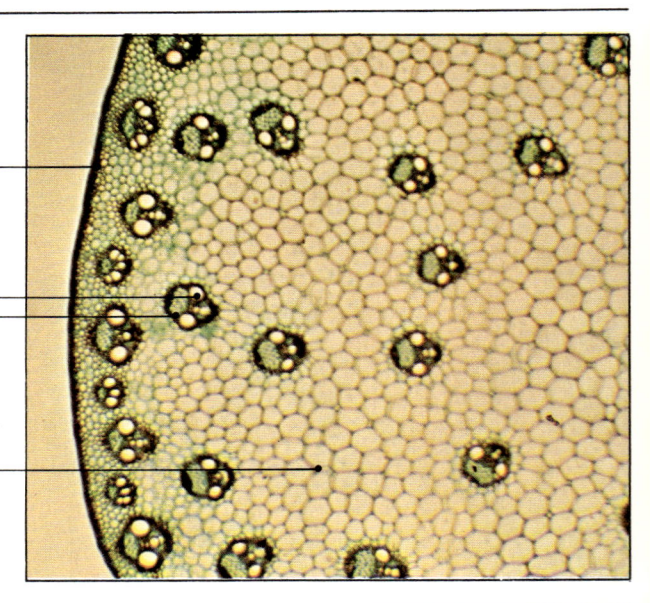

Right: The annual rings can be seen on the cut ends of these larch trees. By counting annual rings on a tree trunk or stump you can tell the age of the tree.

sperm and therefore supply the growing plant with food. But they never take part in photosynthesis. The first green leaves are produced by the plumule. The single cotyledon of a maize seed also remains below the ground, even though the endosperm is outside the cotyledon.

Growing stems and roots

As a plant grows, its stem, branches and roots get longer. At the same time the whole plant becomes thicker and stronger. Growth occurs in special regions called meristems. The increase in the length of stems and branches occurs by growth of meristems in the buds. The tip of a root is also a meristem, and it is here that root growth occurs.

Inside a bud there is a region of dividing cells. As the cells divide, new cells are formed. The region of dividing cells thus moves forward, leaving behind some of the new cells. Further back from the tip of the meristem there is a region of differentiation — a region where cells become different from each other. They alter according to the function they must perform. For example, the cells on the outside of the meristem

---

the cuckoo-pint. This monocotyledon grows in northern temperate regions. It has an ingenious method of preventing self-pollination (see text).

Magnolia is a genus of evergreen and deciduous trees. Originally from Asia and North America, they are now widely planted in temperate regions. They have large, showy flowers, which may be pink, white, yellow or greenish.

Maple (*Acer*) is a genus of 60 species of deciduous trees found widely throughout the Northern Hemisphere. They all produce 2-winged fruits. The leaves of the sugar maple (*A. saccharum*) of North America provide maple sugar. Other maples are popular garden trees. The sycamore (*A. pseudoplatanus*) is native to Europe. The Japanese maple (*A. palmatum*) has leaves that turn bright red in autumn. One of the tallest maples is the North American red maple (*A. rubrum*), which may grow to a height of over 35 metres.

Monoecious plant is a plant that has separate male and female flowers on the same plant. See also DIOECIOUS.

Nettle (*Urtica*) is a genus of 30 species of herbaceous plants. They have stinging hairs on their leaves. The stings of a few Indonesian species can be fatal. Stinging nettles are wind-pollinated and thus their flowers are greenish and indistinct. Deadnettles (*Lamium*) and hemp-nettles (*Galeopsis*) belong to a separate family and do not sting. They can be distinguished from stinging nettles by their purple or white flowers.

Nightshade family contains about 1,800 species of plants. Some of these are useful to man, such as the potato, tomato, aubergine (egg-plant) and sweet pepper. However, others are very poisonous, such as deadly nightshade (*Atropa*

Ancient oak in winter

Passion flowers and fruit

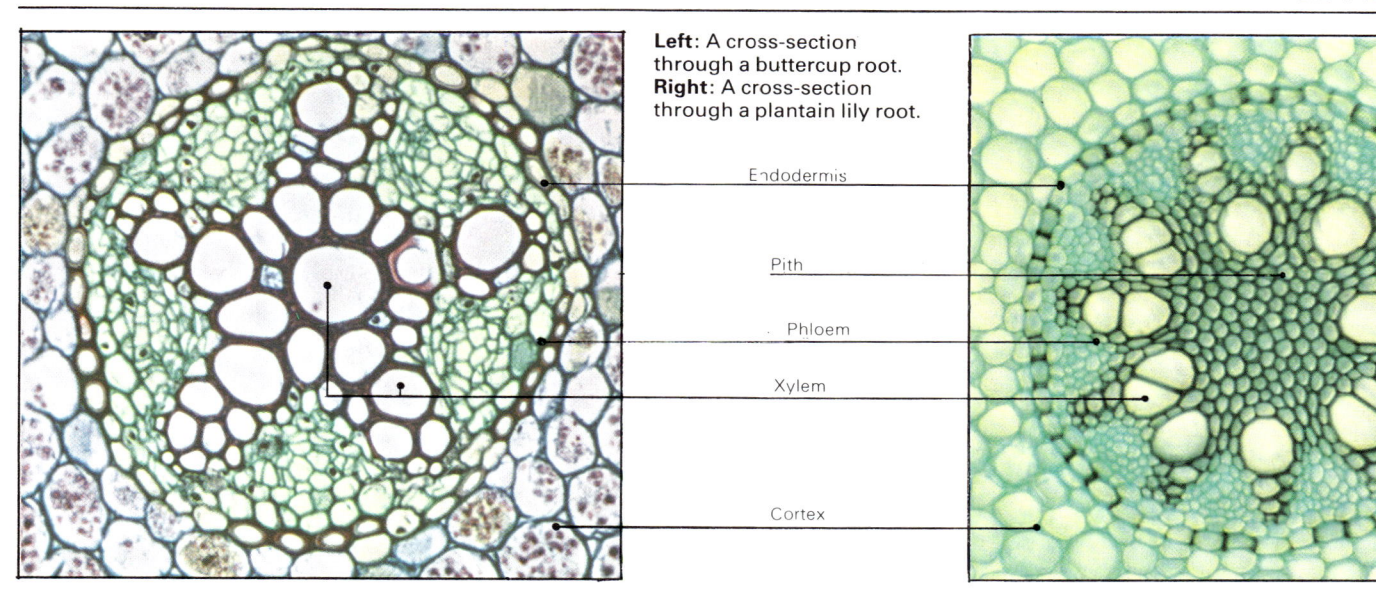

Left: A cross-section through a buttercup root.
Right: A cross-section through a plantain lily root.

- Endodermis
- Pith
- Phloem
- Xylem
- Cortex

become epidermal cells. Others become xylem, phloem or parenchyma cells (*see pages 8-10*).

The same process occurs in the tip of a root but here the region of dividing cells is protected by a covering of tough cells, called the root cap. This is needed because the root meristem would otherwise be damaged as it pushes down through the soil.

In fully-formed stems and roots the cells have become arranged in tissues. These are regions of a plant that have particular functions. For example, all the xylem vessels are arranged together into a water-conducting tissue, called simply the xylem.

The outside of a young stem is covered by the epidermis. Inside this is a region called the cortex, which may consist of parenchyma or collenchyma cells. The phloem and xylem are arranged together in bundles, called vascular bundles. In dicotyledons these vascular bundles form a ring inside the stem, and each bundle consists of phloem on the outside and xylem inside. In monocotyledons the vascular bundles are arranged at random. In the centre of the stem is an area called the pith, or medulla. This is usually made up of parenchyma cells.

The tissues of a root are arranged slightly differently. As in the stem there is an epidermis (called the piliferous layer) and a cortex but the xylem and phloem are placed in the centre of the root. The xylem is arranged like a star, with the phloem placed between the points.

Making wood and bark

If you look at the stump of a tree that has been cut down, you can usually see that it seems to be made up of rings. In fact, each ring represents the growth that took place in a single year. Thus, if you can count the rings you can tell the age of the tree when it was cut.

Each year's growth is due to the activity of yet another meristem (growth region) called the cambium. This is a layer of cells that forms a cylinder inside the stem of the woody plant. As the cells of the cambium divide, new xylem cells are formed inside the cylinder. These tough, thick-walled cells make up the wood of a tree. In the spring the cambium forms large xylem cells. As summer passes the new xylem cells become smaller until, in the autumn, the cambium stops producing cells altogether. Therefore, the rings that you see on a tree stump are made by the difference in appearance between the small autumn cells and the large spring cells.

The cambium also produces new phloem cells on the outside, but these are not as strong as xylem cells. As a result, each year's growth of phloem cells eventually becomes crushed, and so rings are not formed outside the cambium.

The epidermis that covers the outside of a young stem is not strong enough to protect a tree. Therefore, a layer of cells inside the epidermis begins to divide. This layer is known as the cork cambium. The new cells that are produced on the outside of this layer become thick-walled cork

---

belladona), woody nightshade (*Solanum dulcamara*), black nightshade (*Solanum nigrum*) and henbane (*Hyoscyamus niger*). The tobacco plant (*Nicotiana tabacum*) is also a member of this family.
Non-endospermic seed is a seed in which the endosperm (food store) is contained in the COTYLEDONS.
Nut is a one-seeded, INDEHISCENT FRUIT with a woody PERICARP. Examples include hazelnuts, sweet chestnuts, oak acorns and beechnuts. *Note:* some structures are incorrectly regarded as nuts. Coconuts and walnuts are the stones of DRUPES; Brazilnuts are seeds that come from a many-seeded, hard fruit (usually regarded as a BERRY); peanuts are seeds that come from a 2-seeded fruit.

O Oak (*Quercus*) is a genus of over 300 species of deciduous and evergreen trees. They are fine-looking trees, often with massive trunks, and may grow to over 30 metres high. Some of them are important timber trees, for example the North American white oak (*Q. alba*) and the English oak (*Q. robur*). Most of the large oak forests of England were cut down in the 1600s to build ships and houses. The cork oak (*Q. suber*) is the main source of cork, which makes up its spongy bark.
Old man's beard, see CLEMATIS.
Orchids are a family of nearly 20,000 species of monocotyledons. They are found in all parts of the world except the coldest and driest regions, but most orchids are found in tropical areas. They have a distinctive flower structure in which one petal is extended to form a lip. Many orchids are epiphytes (*see page 51*). Many orchids, including the few British species,

Plantains

Poplar

Flowering Plants

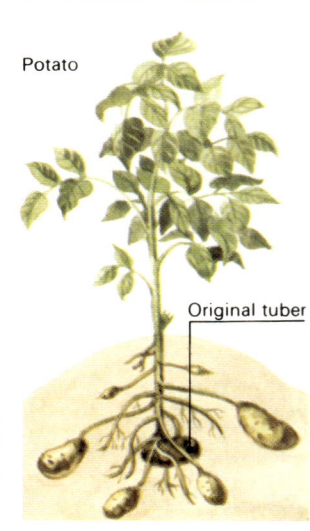

Above: Many plants can reproduce without using flowers. Some cacti produce growths, called mammillae, at their base. Strawberry plants produce long stems called runners. Irises grow from underground stems called rhizomes. Daffodils grow from storage organs called bulbs, which produce new bulbs each year. Crocuses grow from corms, which also produce new corms every year. Potatoes produce underground tubers. These are food storage organs and each one can grow into a new potato plant.

cells, and form the bark of the tree.

Other ways of multiplying

The process of producing a seed involves sex cells. This is the most important way in which flowering plants reproduce, as it results in strong, healthy plants. Also, new varieties may be produced, and eventually new species may evolve.

However, there are various ways in which new plants are formed without sex cells being involved. Various parts of plants are specially modified for this purpose. Usually, it is the stem that is modified.

Rhizomes, such as those of the IRIS, grow underground. They are not roots, they are modified stems. They grow horizontally under the soil. At intervals they grow shoots, which develop into the visible parts of the plants. The rhizomes of the potato plant are much thinner but at certain points they swell up into food storage organs called tubers. Shoots spring up from little buds, called 'eyes', on the surface of the tuber and roots grow from other 'eyes'. The shoots develop into a bushy plant which sends out side stalks close to the surface where new tubers develop.

Runners, such as those of the strawberry plant, are also modified stems. But they grow above the soil. Where they touch the ground new roots are formed. When the new plant is established, the runner withers away. Gardeners find this a useful way of growing new strawberry plants.

Bulbs, such as DAFFODILS, are also modified stems. In fact the true stem is only the solid heart of the bulb. The rest of the bulb is made up of fleshy leaves. New bulbs grow from one or two of the buds that form where the leaves join the stem. A corm, such as that of a CROCUS, is similar to a bulb but it consists mainly of a swollen stem. The leaves are reduced to scales. At the end of the year the old corm dies and a new corm grows above it. At the same time the old corm may produce one or two smaller new corms. Corms and the leaves of bulbs are also food storage organs. The food is used to help the new growth of the plant in spring.

The good-luck plant (*Bryophyllum*) has an

---

are rare and therefore no orchids should be picked.

Palms are a family of about 3,500 species of monocotyledons found in the tropics and sub-tropics. Many species are important to man, including the coconut palm (*Cocos nucifera*), the date palm (*Phoenix dactylifera*), the West African oil palm (*Elaeis guineensis*), and the Malaysian sugar palm (*Arenga saccharifera*).
Pansy, see VIOLET.
Passion flower (*Passiflora*) is a genus of more than 300 species of climbing plants, originally from the tropical regions of America. These plants got their name because their flowers were thought to represent the passion of Christ. Inside the brightly coloured sepals and petals there is a ring of thread-like filaments, and the 3 stigmas are arranged in the shape of a cross.
Pea family is a family of over 7,000 species of plants. They have butterfly-like flowers and produce their seeds in pods. Members of this family include ACACIA, *Mimosa*, LABURNUM, GORSE, peas and beans.

Perennials are plants that continue to grow from year to year. HERBACEOUS perennials die down during the winter and produce new

Rowan tree in flower

growth from their underground parts in the spring. Woody perennials have permanent woody parts above ground all year round. See also ANNUALS, BIENNIALS.
Perianth is the CALYX (sepals) and COROLLA (petals) of a flower. This term is generally used to describe the outer parts of flowers in which the petals and sepals are difficult to tell apart; e.g. the flowers of tulips, irises and lilies.
Pericarp is the outer layers of a fruit, all derived from the wall of the original ovary.
Pink family is a family of over 1,000 species of herbaceous plants. They include carnations, pinks and sweet williams, which all belong to the genus *Dianthus*. Also included are the campions (*Silene*), stitchworts (*Stellaria*), and chickweeds (*Cerastium*). Their flowers are pink or white.
Plane (*Platanus*) is a genus of 6 species of deciduous trees. They are often planted in towns and cities because they are resistant to smoke and fumes.
Plantain (*Plantago*) is a genus of herbaceous plants

Flowering Plants

Right: Many climbing plants are assisted by tendrils. Young tendrils grow straight until they touch a support. If they do not find a support, they eventually coil up and are not used. After a tendril has coiled round a support, the part of the tendril nearest the plant coils in the opposite direction to the part nearest the support. This creates tension and draws the plant and the support closer together.

Below: Plants always grow towards the light. Even if this pot were turned round the seedlings would bend back towards the light. This movement is called phototropism.

unusual way of producing new plants. Along the edges of its leaves it grows tiny plants called bulbils. These fall off, and each one can grow into a new plant.

All these ways in which plants reproduce are called vegetative propagation, and they occur naturally. But man has invented some artificial methods of producing new plants from old ones. The simplest of these is called taking a cutting. A small shoot can be cut from a young stem and planted in soil. After some time it may grow new roots. Chrysanthemums, geraniums and lupins are just three of the many plants from which successful cuttings can be taken. Woody shoots, such as those from rambling roses and gooseberry bushes, can also be treated in the same way. Some plants, such as Begonias, will grow from leaf cuttings.

However, a number of plants cannot be grown from cuttings. In such cases, gardeners use another method called grafting. For example, new fruit trees can be grown from grafted twigs. First, a young, healthy sapling is selected. This is often a wild variety. The main stem is cut off just

found all over the world. They have small, colourless flowers on long spikes. Because plantains will grow in all soils and locations, they are often troublesome weeds on paths and lawns.
Pod, see LEGUME.
Poplar (*Populus*) is a genus of about 35 species of deciduous trees related to the WILLOWS. They are found all over the Northern Hemisphere. Their male and female catkins are borne on separate trees. This genus also includes the aspens and American cottonwoods.
Poppies are a family of about 450 species of herbaceous plants found in sub-tropical and northern temperate regions. British species include the field poppy, or corn poppy (*Papaver rhoeas*), and the yellow horned poppy (*Glaucium flavum*) which grows by the sea.
Primrose (*Primula vulgaris*) is a herbaceous plant that flowers in spring. It grows in woods, hedgerows and grassy places. Pink, purple or white varieties, as well as the pale yellow type, occur.
Privet (*Ligustrum vulgare*) is an almost evergreen shrub found all over Europe. Its white clusters of flowers have an unpleasant smell, and its black berries are poisonous to eat.

Snowdrop

R **Rhododendron** is a genus of over 500 shrubs that come from East Asia. They are all evergreen, except for one group known as azaleas. They have brightly coloured flowers, which are often scented. They are popular shrubs for parks and gardens, but they will not grow in lime-rich soils.
Rose family is a family of about 2,000 species of trees, shrubs and herbaceous plants. Members of this family include plums (*Prunus*), apples (*Malus*), hawthorn (*Crataegus*), blackberry (*Rubus*), and strawberry (*Potentilla*), as well as the true roses (*Rosa*). The 150 species of wild rose are mostly found in the Northern Hemisphere.
Rowan tree (*Sorbus aucuparia*) is a deciduous tree, also called the mountain ash, found in the Northern Hemisphere. It has bright orange-red berries in the autumn.

S **Sapwood** is the outer ring of wood surrounding the HEARTWOOD of a tree. It contains some living cells, as well as xylem cells, and conducts water up the tree.

Flowering Plants

above the roots. The rootstock that remains will form the roots of the new tree. A twig from a tree of the desired variety is then inserted into the bark at the top of the rootstock. This twig grows and eventually forms the flowers and fruit that the gardener requires.

ROSES are propagated by a special method of grafting, called budding. In this case, instead of a twig, a bud is inserted into the top of the rootstock.

Plant movements

Though plants do not move from place to place, certain movements do occur, and they are all concerned with the need for water, food, light, protection or support.

If you grow some seeds indoors near a window, you will find that all the seedlings lean towards the light. Even if you turn the container round, within a few hours the seeds will bend back towards the window. This movement is called phototropism. Because plants must have light in order to make food, they have developed a system that enables them to detect and grow towards a source of light.

A stem always grows upwards, and a root always grows downwards. You can prove this by taking a bean seedling that has already produced a shoot and root. Turn it upside down so that the stem points downwards. Within a few days the root will have curled downwards, and the shoot will have turned so that it once again grows upwards. You can do this in the dark, so that phototropism is not the cause. In fact it is gravity that the plant responds to, and the movement is called geotropism. This is an important movement because it ensures that the root of a seedling grows down into the soil where there are minerals and water. At the same time the shoot grows up through the soil, eventually reaching the light.

There are a number of other plant movements. Some flowers, such as those of the DAISY, open during the day and close at night. Crocus flowers open only when the temperature rises above a certain point. Some climbing plants have tendrils that grow out in spirals. When a tendril finds a support, it quickly coils round it. Some bean plants of the genus Vicia have a 'sleep movement' – a raising and lowering of the leaves from the horizontal during the day to the vertical at night.

One of the most spectacular plant movements is shown by *Mimosa*. During the day the leaves are erect, but at night the plant appears to wilt. This sleep movement can also be made to happen by giving the plant a sharp knock. The leaves collapse suddenly, due to a very rapid change in turgor pressure (*see page 10*).

Above and below: *Mimosa* is a plant that has sleep movements. In the normal position *(above)* the leaflets are erect. In the sleep position *(below)* the leaflets are folded down. This normally occurs in the evening, but a sudden tap can cause it in the day.

Schizocarp is a fruit that breaks into several pieces, which are generally one-seeded. Examples include the fruits of *Geranium*, dead-nettles, and hemlock.
Shrub is a woody plant that has several stems arising from the soil. See also TREE.
Snapdragon, see ANTIRRHINUM.
Snowdrop (*Galanthus*) is a genus of 13 species of monocotyledons found in Europe and the Middle East. They grow from bulbs and have bell-shaped flowers.
Sunflower (*Helianthus annuus*) is an annual herbaceous plant related to the daisy. The flower heads have many brown disc-florets surrounded by a ring of large, yellow ray-florets.

Thistles are a group of herbaceous plants related to the daisy. Their flower heads are made up of purple, tubular disc-florets. British species include the common field thistle (*Cirsium arvense*), the marsh thistle (*C. palustre*), the slender thistle (*Carduus tenuiflorus*), and the Scotch thistle (*Onopordum acanthium*).
Tree is a woody plant that

Scotch thistle

has a single stem arising from the soil. *See also* SHRUB.
Tulip (*Tulipus*) is a large genus of monocotyledons that mainly come from Asia and the Mediterranean region. They grow from bulbs, and their petals and sepals are alike. Since the 1500s many garden varieties have been bred.
Tulip tree (*Liriodendron tulipifera*) is a deciduous tree from North America. It is related to the magnolias and has large, greenish flowers.

Vines are a family of climbing plants, mostly from tropical and sub-tropical regions. They include the grape (*Vitis vinifera*).
Violet (*Viola*) is a genus of herbaceous plants that includes the pansies. There are about 400 species, mostly small herbaceous plants. They grow all over the world.

Willow (*Salix*) is a genus of about 170 deciduous trees found all over the world. They are graceful trees, and the Chinese weeping willow (*S. babylonica*) is a popular garden variety.

Plants have adapted to cope with all kinds of climates: hot and cold, dry and swampy, salt water and fresh water. Each plant is suited to its own environment and this accounts for the enormous variety of plant life on the Earth.

Adaptation to Environment

Left: Mangroves have stilt roots to support them in the swampy ground in which they grow. This genus (*Rhizophora*) has breathing pores in the bends of the stilts to provide oxygen to the roots below.
Below: Air spaces in the leaves and stem of a water lily help the leaves to float. They also help to supply oxygen to the plant.

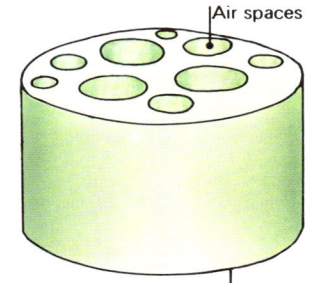

Plants need water and food to survive no matter where they live. In most temperate climates these are present in suitable amounts. Therefore, it is relatively easy for plants to take in what they need. The adaptations of plants to such environments are those that we accept as the normal plant structures – a standard root, stem and leaf system.

However, there are climates that are less hospitable. For example, water may be scarce, or there may be too much of it. The plants that live in normal environments cannot survive under such conditions. However, plants, and particularly flowering plants, are very adaptable. Many of them have evolved ways of overcoming hardships. Thus even the inhospitable environments of the world have their own particular plant populations.

Living in water
Since water is essential for plants, it may seem surprising that a plant can have too much water. After all, algae spend all their lives in water and have no problems. Ferns, gymnosperms and flowering plants are basically land plants which evolved from plants that established themselves on land millions of years ago. Only more recently have some of them returned to a watery environment – like the whales in the animal kingdom.

A land plant needs to have a strong stem for support but an aquatic (water) plant is held up by the water around it. Thus, one of the characteristics of such plants is the reduction of the stem tissues. They have few fibres and little or no xylem. Instead, they have air spaces that help to keep them floating in the water. These air

Reference

A **Alpine zones** occur on mountains below the permanent snow fields and above the timber line. This type of climate is cold and harsh and supports only hardy, low-growing plants.
Amazonian water lily (*Victoria amazonica*) is the largest of all the water lilies; its leaves may be up to 150 cm across, and its flowers are about 30 cm across.
American century plant (*Agave americana*) is a North American desert plant. It has long, tapering, fleshy leaves covered in a tough cuticle. It gets its name from the fact that it may take over 50 years to flower.
American resurrection plant (*Selaginella lepidophylla*) is a clubmoss (see page 30) that can withstand being completely dried out. Although it appears to be rolled up and dead, when moistened it unrolls and revives. It is often sold as a curiosity.
Azolla is a fern that grows in water. The undersides of its fronds are covered in special hairs that repel water. As a result the fronds float, and dense mats of this fern can cover ponds. The fronds turn red in the autumn.

B **Banyan** (*Ficus*) is a genus of Asian and African plants related to the fig. Banyans begin life as EPIPHYTES on palm trees. They put down aerial roots, which eventually reach the soil. The roots are able to fuse together round the host tree. Finally, the host is strangled, and the banyan remains, a tree with a 'trunk' made of aerial roots. Banyans also spread from tree to tree along the branches, putting down aerial roots all the time.
Bindweed see page 37.
Bird's nest orchid (*Neottia nidus-avis*) is a plant whose leaves contain little or no

Amazonian water lily

Adaptation to Environment

Below: Water milfoil *(Myriophyllum)* has two kinds of leaves. Underwater leaves are long and narrow so that they can withstand water currents and provide a maximum surface for taking in dissolved gases. The leaves above the water have stomata, and more woody tissue for support.

spaces also perform another function. They help oxygen to reach the underwater parts of the plants.

Submerged plants in rivers, like the Canadian pondweed, have to survive the battering they receive from the water currents. To do this they have flexible stems and long, thin leaves. Water currents pass smoothly over these plants, and the leaves do not tear.

Aquatic plants with floating leaves have the problem of avoiding damage by wind and waves. The best-known of these plants are the water lilies. They have circular leaves, and scientists think that this is probably the best design for avoiding the possibility of being torn or swamped by waves. The largest example of this type of plant is the giant AMAZONIAN WATER LILY, whose leaves may be one and a half metres across. They are reinforced by stiff ridges underneath and are strong enough to take the weight of a child.

There are many other plants with floating leaves and they are generally found in sheltered ponds, where damage is less likely to occur. Some of them, such as the duckweeds, are free-floating. A single duckweed plant consists merely of a simple leaf-like body and one or more hanging roots. WOLFFIA, the smallest of all the flowering plants (less than half a millimetre across), consists of a tiny round body with no roots, stem or leaves.

Plants with parts above the water may be little different to land plants, particularly if they live in only shallow water. The common reed is an ordinary monocotyledon. However, plants that live in deeper water may have more complicated structures. MANGROVES live in coastal swamps. They have tall, arching stilt roots that keep the main parts of the plant clear of the high tide mark, whereas their roots are buried in mud that contains little oxygen. Therefore, they have specialized roots called pneumatophores that project above the mud and water to get oxygen from the air.

Living in salty conditions

The problem of a plant that lives near the sea or an inland salt lake is how to get the water it needs. It is a problem because the water outside the plant contains a high concentration of salt (and is therefore a strong solution). Osmosis, the process by which plants take in water, works by moving water from a weak solution to a strong solution (*see page 11*).

The simplest way to overcome this problem is to ensure that the cell sap is stronger than even the salty water outside. Thus osmosis can still take place. Most plants that live in these conditions have much stronger cell solutions than plants living under normal conditions.

However, there are times when even this does not work. For example, after a storm there may be much more salt than usual in the soil. To

Above: The rhizomes of marram grass help to bind sand dunes together. Marram grass can survive the dry conditions on the dunes because of the structure of its leaves.

---

chlorophyll (green pigment). Hence it cannot make its own food. Many people regard this plant as a saprophyte (feeding on dead organic matter) but in fact it has a mass of short thick roots that are entangled with a fungus. Such a relationship is usually either a symbiosis, or the fungus is a parasite but in this case the orchid relies on the fungus to break down the organic matter on which it lives. It cannot do this by itself, and it can therefore be said to parasitize the fungus.
Bladderworts *(Utricularia)* are carnivorous plants found in water and in damp places, particularly in tropical regions. They have tiny bladders that trap small animals. Each bladder is closed by a small valve. Inside the bladder there is a slight vacuum. When an animal disturbs the hairs around the opening, the valve flies open and the animal is sucked into the bladder. The valve closes and the animal dies in the bladder. Gradually, the animal is digested, and this process helps to create a new vacuum inside the bladder. Thus the trap is re-set.

Bird's nest orchid

Bindweed *see page 57.*
Bromeliads are a family of monocotyledonous South American plants, many of which are EPIPHYTES. Some of them catch water in cups formed by the wide bases of their leaves.
Broomrapes *(Orobanche)* are a genus of parasitic plants found in Europe, Asia and Africa. Their leaves contain no chlorophyll and their tubers are attached to the roots of host plants, such as clovers, peas and daisies.
Butterworts *(Pinguicula)* are a genus of carnivorous plants. They have small rosettes of leaves covered with a butter-coloured, sticky substance that traps insects.

Cactus (plural: cacti) is a member of the family Cactaceae. They are all succulent plants with modified stems for withstanding drought conditions. Their leaves are modified into spines, hairs or bristles.
Californian poppy *(Eschscholtzia californica)* is an EPHEMERAL desert plant found in North America.
Canadian pond weed *(Elodea canadensis)* is a

Adaptation to Environment 51

Above: After a rainstorm this area of desert in Central Australia is blooming with ephemeral (short-lived) flowers.
Left: The filamentous alga *Spirogyra* forms a green scum on the surface of a sheltered pond. The lesser duckweed (*Lemna minor*) floats on the surface, together with the reddish leaves of the water fern *Azolla*.

Right: The glasswort (*Salicornia*), with its fleshy leaves, can live in the salty waters of an estuary.

overcome this many seaside plants, such as the glassworts, have fleshy leaves that store water. In this way they can survive until the concentration of salt around them becomes low enough again.

Living in dry conditions
The deserts provide some of the harshest climates to be found in the world. Some places, such as the middle of the Sahara desert, are so dry that nothing can live there. However, given even a little water some plants can survive, using their special adaptations.

The simplest way to combat drought is to avoid it altogether. Parts of some deserts are subject to long periods of drought, followed by sudden short periods of torrential rain. During the drought, few plants appear to be present. But immediately after the rain a large number of plants emerge from seeds that have been lying

North American water plant, now abundant in Britain. It grows completely submerged and its elongated leaves are borne on long, flexible stems.
Candle plant (*Kleinia articulata*) is a stem succulent related to the daisy. In times of drought it loses its few leaves and survives on the water stored in its swollen stem.
Creosote bush (*Covillea glutinosa*) is a North American desert plant. It looks like an ordinary plant, but it is able to withstand drought because its cells can still carry out their work when they have lost water.

D Deserts are areas of land that receive little or no rain. Some are permanently hot, such as the Sahara desert in North Africa but the northern deserts of Asia are extremely cold at night and during the winter.
Dodder (*Cuscuta*) is a genus of parasitic plants found in many parts of the world. They are parasites of clovers, hops, nettles, gorse and heather, and may cause damage to crops.
Duckweed (*Lemna*) is a genus of small free-floating water plants found on ponds, ditches and lakes all over the world.

E Eelgrass (*Zostera*) is one of the few water plants (except for seaweeds) that lives in the sea. It is submerged and even produces underwater flowers.
Ephemeral plants are those that only live for a very short period of time – just long enough to flower and produce seeds.
Epiphytes are plants that grow on other plants. They are not parasites, they only use their hosts for support.

G Glasswort (*Salicornia*) is a succulent plant that lives near the sea in salty conditions.

H Halophytes are plants that grow in salty soil.
Honeysuckle see page 41.

Cacti in France

Stony desert

52 Adaptation to Environment

dormant. These are called ephemeral plants. They grow, flower and produce seeds in a very short time, before the heat kills them. The new seeds remain in the soil, waiting for the next rainstorm.

Some plants are able to endure the loss of water in dry conditions. The CREOSOTE BUSH, which is found in the deserts of North America, looks like a normal plant but its cells can withstand being dried out. The AMERICAN RESURRECTION PLANT is another curious example. In dry conditions it rolls up and appears dead but when it becomes moist again it unrolls. Many mosses are also able to withstand drying out. *Tortula muralis*, for example, a common wall moss in Britain, revives rapidly after a shower of rain.

However, most plants cannot endure water loss, and so those that live in dry conditions have to have some means of preventing it. The first and most obvious step to take is to reduce the rate of transpiration. MARRAM GRASS, which grows on sand dunes and is common in Britain, has an excellent method of doing this. Its leaves are covered with a tough epidermis. They are also curled, and the stomata are situated in pits. A moist atmosphere is thus created above the stomata, and transpiration is slowed down.

Plants in hotter climates require more drastic measures, and the best-known desert plants are those that store water – the cacti and other succulents. Some of these succulents store water in their leaves, such as the pebble-plants ('living stones') and the AMERICAN CENTURY PLANT.

Above: These cacti flourish in the deserts of the American continent. They are all adapted to living in dry, arid conditions and have fleshy stems or leaves for water storage. Some have brightly coloured flowers which attract insect pollinators.

Hydrophytes are plants that grow in water.

I **Ivy** see page 42.

L **Lianas** are climbing plants found in tropical forests. They have woody stems. Some climb by twining round trees. Others use tendrils, or thorns.

M **Mangroves** include several shrubs that belong to 3 different families. However, they all have stilt roots and pneumatophores (adaptations for life in tidal mudflats).

Marram grass (*Ammophila arenaria*) grows on raised sand dunes and cannot tolerate immersion in the sea (unlike SEA COUCHGRASS). The binding action of its roots and rhizomes cause larger dunes to build up. Eventually the dunes become more stable and contain more humus (from dead marram grass). At this stage marram grass is succeeded by other plants. Sand dunes contain very little water, and marram grass is adapted to these dry conditions. Its curled leaves and sunken stomata help to slow the transpiration rate.

Mistletoe is a partial parasite of trees. The common mistletoe is usually found on apple trees. In some parts of the world mistletoe can be a serious tree pest.

O **Old man of the desert** (*Cephalocereus senilis*) is a Mexican cactus that has silvery, hair-like outgrowths instead of spines.

P **Papyrus** (*Cyperus papyrus*) is a reed-like water plant found in Africa. It is normally rooted beneath the water, but sometimes forms vast floating rafts. In ancient Egypt papyrus was used for building and papermaking.

Parasite is a plant or animal that lives at the expense of another plant or animal, without giving anything in return.

Adaptation to Environment

Others, such as cacti and the candle plant, use their stems as storage organs. The main purpose of the shape of these plants is to reduce the surface area exposed to the drying air. The outer layers of succulents are tough, and there are few stomata. As a result the rate of transpiration is very slow. In this way some cacti can survive for several years without water.

The bristles and spines of cacti are a further adaptation. They are actually modified leaves, and they serve to discourage animals in search of a juicy meal. The bristles of the prickly pear cactus break off easily and act like itching powder.

Living with other plants

The majority of plants live more or less independently, although members of a plant community may get some benefit from each other, such as protection. Most of the plants in such a community make their own food and support themselves. However, some plants cheat and allow others to do some or all of the work for them. Such plants are specially adapted for obtaining their food or support, or both of these from other plants.

Sometimes two plants may live in a close association that is beneficial to both plants. Each one provides something that the other needs. This kind of relationship is called symbiosis. Many fungi form symbiotic relationships (*see page 25*). For example in a lichen, the fungus gains food from the alga, and the alga gets protection

Below: A cactus survives in the desert because it stores water in its stem. The spines, which are modified leaves, protect it from animals.

Above: *Lithops bella*, a pebble plant, stores water in its leaves. It is overlooked by animals because of its resemblance to pebbles.

Below: The creosote bush can survive in places where no other plants exist. Its cells are able to withstand being dried out.

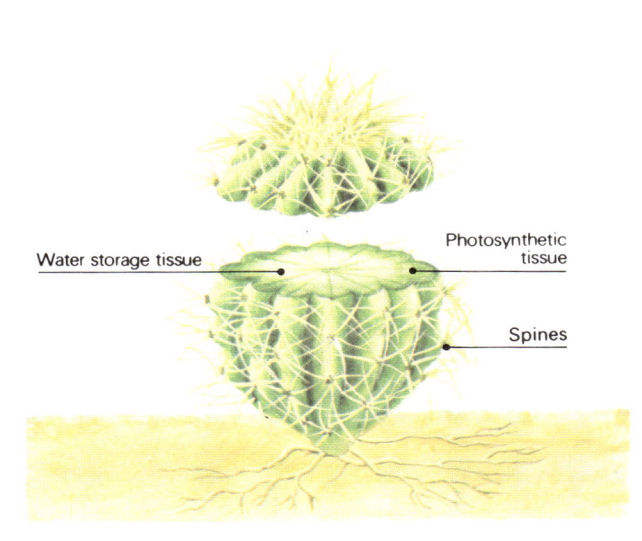

Pebble plants ('living stones') are a number of different plants that mimic pebbles. They have one or two pairs of fleshy leaves.
Pitcher plant (*Nepenthes*) is a genus of 67 species of tropical, carnivorous plants, mostly found in Malaysia. Some species have creeping rhizomes in swampy ground, and their pitchers lie in the leaf litter of the forest. Others are EPIPHYTES, living high in the trees. Pitchers are formed at the end of the plant's long leaves. Insects are attracted to a pitcher by the nectar produced by the lid, which also keeps out the rain. Some species of pitcher plant are brightly coloured, and this also helps to attract insects. When an insect lands at the top of a pitcher, it cannot hold on to the slippery surface. It therefore falls into the liquid below, where it is digested. Sometimes a crab spider may occupy the upper part of a pitcher, taking a share of the victims as they arrive.
Prickly pear cactus (*Opuntia*) is a genus of cacti found in most desert conditions. Its fruit ('cactus apples'; 'cactus figs'; 'tunas') is often eaten in poorer areas. Prickly pears have also been used as fodder and to make thick, impenetrable hedges.

Mistletoe berries

Rafflesia is a genus of plants that are parasites of vines in Malaysia and Indonesia. An adult plant consists mostly of threads that penetrate the tissues of the host. Only the flowers are fully developed. In fact, *Rafflesia arnoldii* bears the world's largest flower, which may be over a metre across.
Reedswamp is a dense community of plants found along the edges of rivers and lakes. It is mostly composed of 2 water plants, the common reed (*Phragmites*) and the reedmace (*Typha*). The common reed is a grass.

Reeds

The reedmace is a monocotyledon with long, sword-like leaves and dense, dark brown spikes of flowers.

Adaptation to Environment

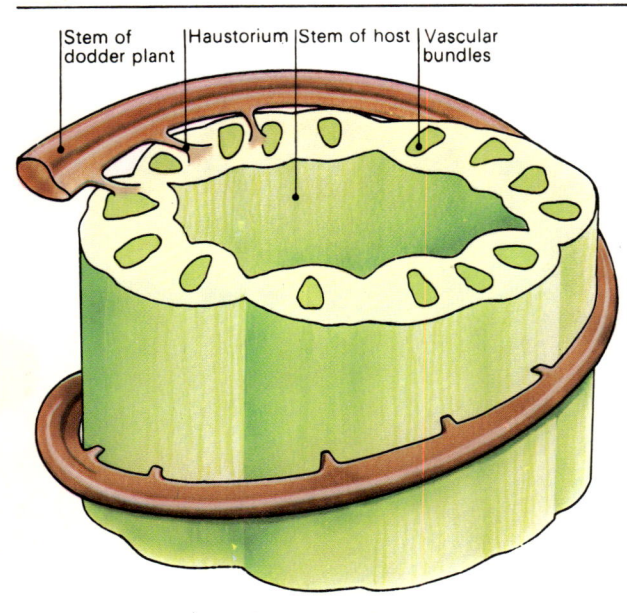

Above: Dodder is a total parasite, relying on its host for all its food and water. It coils round and draws food from the host's xylem and phloem.

Below: Mistletoe is only a partial parasite. It takes water and some food from its host, but its leaves are green and are able to photosynthesize.

Below: A Chinese banyan *(Ficus retusa)* has a large 'trunk' made of aerial roots. As the branches grow outwards, more aerial roots are put down.

from bright light and water loss. The symbiosis of a fungus with the roots of a flowering plant is called a mycorrhiza. The fungus takes sugar from the roots, and the flowering plant benefits because the fungus is more efficient in absorbing water and minerals from the soil.

There are also plants that cheat even more and rely entirely on others for their existence. Such plants are called parasites. There are many examples of parasites among the fungi, but there are also some flowering plant parasites.

MISTLETOE is a parasite of trees. It attaches itself to the branches and takes water from the xylem tissue of the host. It is however only a partial parasite, as it has green leaves and is able to make its own food.

Several flowering plants are total parasites. For example, DODDER is a parasite of clover, nettles, hops, gorse, and heather. In America one species twines itself round the stems of lucerne and alfalfa and makes these crops difficult to harvest. When a dodder seed germinates, it first puts down a small root. Then the shoot grows rapidly upwards. If it finds a host, the shoot curls

Saguaro cactus *(Carnegiea gigantica)* is a very large cactus that forms forests in the deserts of Arizona, USA.
Salvinia is a fern that lives in water. Its leaves form star-shaped patterns on the surface of the water. It is kept afloat by air trapped in between tiny hairs on its undersurface. *Salvinia* has no roots, but feathery leaves hang down below the surface of the water. It originated in Central and South America, but is now established in Central Africa and Sri Lanka, where it is a serious problem. It grows rapidly, forming dense mats that choke the waterways.
Sarracenia is a genus of 10 species of carnivorous plants found in North America. They are similar to pitcher plants, but their tall, trumpet-shaped pitchers grow directly out of the ground. Insects fall into the liquid inside the pitcher because it is lined with a special epidermis on which they cannot walk. This is the same type of epidermis as the one found lining the flower head of an arum plant (see page 40).

Scarlet pimpernel

Scarlet pimpernel *(Anagallis arvensis)* is a herbaceous plant related to the primrose. It is a common weed found in gardens, fields and roadsides. In such conditions it has normal leaves but when the plant grows in salty conditions, the leaves become succulent. Thus the scarlet pimpernel is an example of a plant that can adapt to the conditions around it.
Sea couchgrass *(Agropyron juncaeum)* is a grass that can tolerate being immersed in sea water. It therefore grows near the edge of the sea. Its deep, extensive system of rhizomes helps to bind the sand together. As a result, small sand dunes form. This is the beginning of natural land reclamation. Sea couchgrass is succeeded by other grasses, particularly MARRAM GRASS.
Sedum is a genus of plants with succulent leaves. It can therefore survive dry conditions. This genus includes the stonecrops and several houseplants grown for their attractive leaves.
Subtropical regions are those where it is warm in both winter and summer.

Adaptation to Environment

round the host's stem and puts out suckers called haustoria. These penetrate the host's tissues, and the dodder plant can then get water and food from the host's xylem and phloem. The root of the dodder plant dies, leaving it completely dependent on its host.

Other flowering plant parasites include BROOMRAPES, TOOTHWORTS and RAFFLESIA, which parasitize the roots of their hosts.

Some plants cheat in the way that they get light for photosynthesis. In a wood or jungle, most plants put a lot of energy into growing thick stems in order to reach the light. Climbing plants, however, save this energy by using other plants for support. They are not parasites, because they have underground roots and green leaves, but they cannot grow properly without the support of trees or walls.

Various methods are used for climbing. The bindweeds curl anticlockwise up the stem of a supporting plant; honeysuckles curl clockwise. Grasping climbers, such as the sweet pea, have tendrils that they use for holding on to their support. The virginia creeper has tendrils with suckers, which stick to the surface over which the plant is climbing. Penetrating climbers, such as ivy, have roots that can grow into the bark of a tree or the surface of a wall. Brambles do not make a positive attempt to climb. But they grow long shoots that fall over when they get too long. The sharp prickles catch on to sturdier plants, and in this way the plants ramble over the surrounding vegetation.

Another group of plants have an even simpler method of getting nearer the light. They grow high up in the branches of trees. Again, they are not parasites because they take no food from the trees. They get their food from rotting leaves and other material trapped in the branches. These plants are called epiphytes. In temperate climates the only epiphytes are mosses and ferns, but in tropical areas, epiphytes include many orchids and BROMELIADS.

The main problem for epiphytes is how to get water. They solve this by putting down aerial roots, which absorb water from the humid air of the tropical forest.

Carnivorous plants

Plants that live in marshy ground, such as peat

Above: A bromeliad is an epiphyte, living high in the branches of trees. It traps water in a central 'tank' and in hollows at the base of its leaves.

Below: The European sundew (Drosera rotundifolia) is a carnivorous plant that traps insects in the sticky fluid exuded from its tentacles.

They extend outside the tropical regions to about 36°S and 36°N.

Succulent plants are those that have swollen, water-storing leaves or stems. Leaf succulents include PEBBLE PLANTS, SEDUM, and the AMERICAN CENTURY PLANT. Stem succulents include cacti and the CANDLE PLANT.

Sundews (Drosera) are 3 species of carnivorous plants with tentacles on their leaves. They grow in places where the soil is poor, such as peat bogs. When an insect lands on a sundew leaf, it is caught by the sticky droplets on the ends of the tentacles. These bend over to hold the insect more firmly against the leaf. They then secrete a liquid that digests the insect. D. rotundifolia has spoon-shaped leaves that spread out near the ground. D. anglica has longer, more tapering leaves on upright stalks. D. intermedia has very long leaves.

Temperate regions are those that have a warm summer and a cold winter. Most temperate land areas are in the Northern Hemisphere and extend from the subtropics to the TUNDRA.

Toothworts (Lathraea) are a genus of parasitic plants found in Europe and Asia. They are related to the BROOMRAPES and are parasitic on the roots of trees. The British species (L. squamaria) is usually found on the roots of hazel or elm trees. It has no surface from which transpiration can take place. The water that it takes up from its host is exuded through special water glands. L. clandestina has no stem above the ground, and some of its bright purple flowers may remain below

Toothwort

the soil.

Tortula muralis is a very common moss on walls. It forms neat cushions, and its leaves are tipped with long, silvery hairs. Its spore capsules are pointed and upright. Its cells are able to withstand water loss. In dry conditions the moss may appear to be dead, but it quickly revives after rain.

Tropical regions extend between 2 lines of latitude – the Tropic of Cancer (23° 27'N) and the Tropic of Capricorn (23° 27'S). In this region the Sun is overhead twice a year, and the weath-

Adaptation to Environment

Above and below: Pitcher plants, such as *Nepenthes madagascariensis*, grow in tropical rain forests, either as epiphytes or in the soil. Insects are attracted by its scent. They cannot hold on to the shiny surface and therefore fall into the fluid at the bottom of the pitcher.

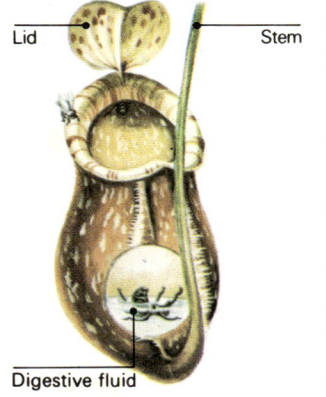

Right: The defences of some nettles are formidable. *Urtica ferox*, from New Zealand, is a woody shrub with large stinging hairs.

bogs, have difficulty in getting all the food they need. Some plants have therefore adapted to this problem by catching and digesting insects. They are thus the killers of the plant world.

There are a variety of techniques that plants use to catch their prey. The most spectacular carnivorous plant is the VENUS FLY TRAP. Its two-lobed leaves are fringed with spikes. When an insect lands on a leaf, the lobes close, trapping the insect inside. A pitcher plant, which may live as an epiphyte or in swampy ground, has a vase-like construction. Insects, attracted by the nectar on the lid, fall into a digestive fluid at the base, from which they cannot escape. The tentacles of a SUNDEW plant are tipped with drops of sticky liquid. These trap any small insects that land on the plant. The leaves of butterworts are completely covered in a sticky substance, which glues the insects down while they are being digested. BLADDERWORTS are plants that trap small water animals in their bladders. The opening of a bladder is closed by a small valve. When an animal touches the hairs round the opening, the valve opens and the animal is sucked in.

Plant defences

Many plants have developed ways of making themselves less attractive to plant-eating animals. Some produce poisons that cause an animal to be sick, and this discourages the animal from eating that plant again. A nettle produces poison in the hairs on its epidermis. A hair injects the poison into anything that touches it, causing the familiar sting. A large number of plants have thorns, spines and prickles to defend them. These also help to reduce water loss.

---

er is always hot (except in ALPINE areas).
Tundra has the world's coldest recorded temperatures. It lies between the northern belt of coniferous trees and the Arctic circle. The main plants are lichens and mosses

V **Venus fly trap** (*Dionaea muscipula*) is a carnivorous plant found in California, USA. Its 2-lobed leaves are fringed with spikes. Also along the edges of the leaves are glands that produce nectar. Inside the spikes, the rest of the leaf is covered by red digestive glands, and each lobe has three trigger hairs. A drop of rain that knocks one hair does not cause anything to happen but when an insect, attracted by the nectar, touches a trigger twice in succession, or touches two hairs, the trap is sprung. The lobes close rapidly, trapping the insect inside the interlocked spikes, where it is digested.

W **Water hyacinth** (*Eichhornia crassipes*) is a water plant that floats because of pockets of air in its leaf bases. It originated in the tropical regions of America, but is now causing serious congestion in many waterways.
Water lilies (*Nymphaea*) are plants with large floating leaves. They have attractive flowers and are much used in ornamental ponds.
Wolffia is the smallest known flowering plant, being only 0.5 to 0.7 mm across. It has no roots, stem or leaves, and consists merely of a tiny round body. Even so, *Wolffia* can cover the entire surface of a sheltered pond.

Venus fly trap

X **Xerophyte** is a plant adapted to life in dry conditions.

Y **Yucca** is a genus of desert plants belonging to the lily family. They are found in Central and South America, where they are known as Joshua trees. Their flowers are pollinated by a particular species of moth. The female moth lays her egg inside the ovary of the flower and then deliberately pollinates it. The moth larva feeds on part of the fruit after it has developed.

All animals, including man, depend on plants for survival. The systematic, scientific cultivation of plants for food has allowed many species to thrive. However, man's progress threatens extinction for many species.

Plants and Man

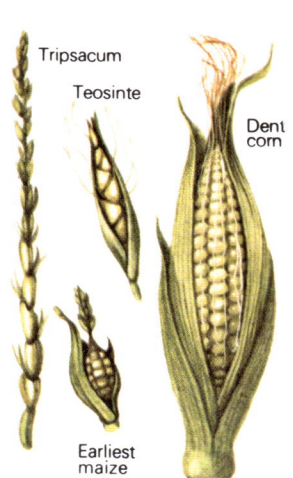

Left: The earliest maize had 48 kernels on each cob. It was cultivated by the Indians of tropical America. They cross-bred early maize with *Tripsacum dactyloides*, a wild grass relative. This produced teosinte (*Euchlaeana mexicana*), which they crossed again with early maize. The resulting larger cobs have since been selectively bred to produce modern maize, such as dent corn, which has 500-1000 kernels on each cob.

Above: The 'wheat triangle' in Montana, USA, is an excellent wheat-growing area. The summers are hot and dry and the winters are cold and wet. Wheat is grown on about 30% of all the land used for grain crops.

Early man was a wanderer. Small groups of people moved from place to place using what food they could find. Then, about 10,000 years ago, man discovered that the plant foods he needed would grow again in the same place from scattered seeds. He also found that he could help these plants to grow by planting the seeds in good soil. At the same time, if he saved the best seeds, the new plants would be stronger and more fruitful. So the descendants of early man settled down and became farmers. By selecting the best of their crops and animals for breeding, they began the process of domestication.

Underground food stores, such as roots, bulbs and tubers were probably the first to be used by man. They are available in almost every part of the world. Even today roots form the main diet for some primitive peoples, such as the few Aborigines that still lead a wandering life in the Australian outback.

We also know that the pods and seeds of legumes (members of the pea family) were being eaten 10,000 years ago. The Indians of Peru ate KIDNEY BEANS 7,000 years ago, and broad beans have been part of the diet of Europeans for over 5,000 years.

The most important part of the early farmers' work was the cultivation of wild grasses. Over a period of thousands of years these grasses have been carefully bred into the modern cereals. Many of the original wild grasses are now extinct, but some still exist, and so we can trace the ways in which modern crops have been produced.

During most of this time the only method of breeding better plants was by selection. Farmers

Reference

A **Adder's tongue spearwort** (*Ranunculus ophioglossifolius*) is a rare British plant related to the buttercup. It is only known in one place — the Badgeworth Nature Reserve, Gloucestershire.
Almond (*Prunus dulcis*) is a small tree cultivated in southern Europe and Western Asia. It is grown for its edible seeds, contained in DRUPES (*see page 39*).
Apples are all derived from the wild crab apple (*Malus pumila*), a tree that grows in Europe, Asia and North America. After centuries of breeding there are now over 3,000 kinds of cultivated apples. The apple fruit is called a pome.
Artichokes are members of the daisy family. Globe artichokes (*Cyanara scolymus*) are closely related to thistles. They are grown for their flower heads, which are edible when immature. Jerusalem artichokes (*Helianthus tuberosus*) are related to the sunflower and are grown for their tubers.
Asparagus (*Asparagus officinalis*) is a member of the lily family grown for its edible young shoots.
Aster is a genus of perennial garden plants. There are a number of hybrids, including the Michaelmas daisy (*A. novibelgii*). 
Aubergine (*Solanum melongena*) is a perennial plant, also called the egg plant, grown for its fruit, which is a glossy, firm berry, either purple or white.
Aubretia is a genus of perennial garden plants with small purple flowers. They are small bushy plants frequently grown on walls or in rock gardens.

Aubergine

B **Banana** (*Musa*) is a genus of giant herbs grown in tropical regions. Cultivated varieties have edible, seedless fruits (berries).
Barley (*Hordeum*) is a genus of 6 species belonging to the grass family. The 3 cultivated species have 2, 4 or 6 rows of grain on the ears. Two-rowed barley is grown in Britain for making beer.
Beetroot (*Beta vulgaris*) is a purple root crop grown in many parts of the world.
Begonia is a large genus of garden and indoor plants. Some species are grown for their leaves, others are

Plants and Man

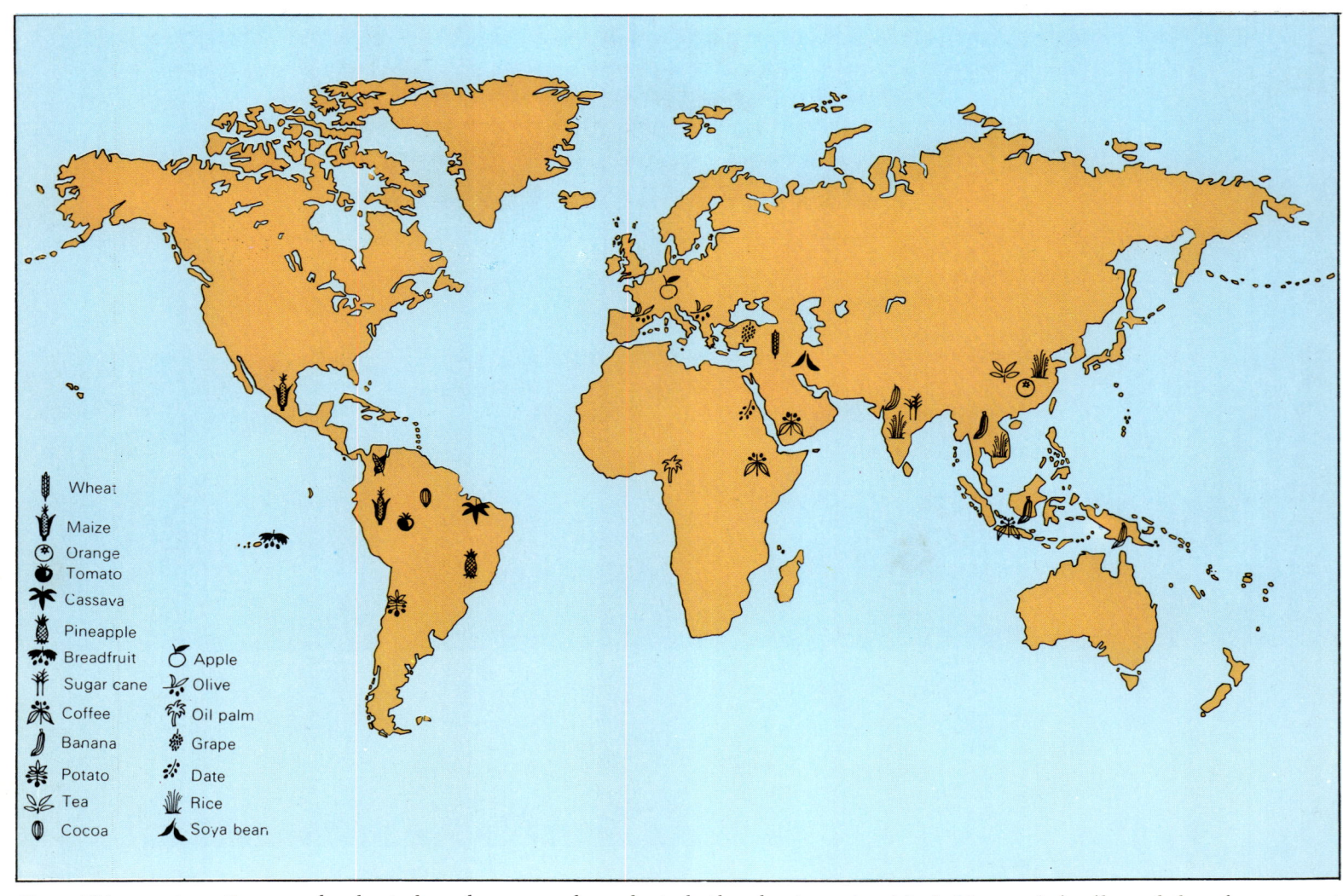

Above: This map shows the origins of some of the world's main food crops. Some crops originated in Europe and Asia, but South America has also produced a large number.

and plant breeders merely selected the best strains and allowed them to grow. For example, MAIZE (sweetcorn) was produced in this way. The original plant had few seeds. By growing seeds from only those plants with the most seeds, farmers eventually produced the many-seeded maize plant grown today.

In the 1700s, scientists began to understand more about heredity – how characteristics are passed on from one generation to the next. Therefore, they could begin to use more scientific methods of producing food crops with better flavours, bigger yields and greater resistance to disease. One way of doing this is to cross-breed two different species. This is known as hybridization, and the plant that results from such a cross is called a hybrid. Many hybrids, particularly animal hybrids, are infertile and therefore cannot be used to produce another generation, though a number of plant hybrids are fertile and are often much stronger than their parents. This strength is called hybrid vigour. Many of our modern cultivated plants, including ROSES, have been produced in this way. Hybrid orchids create spectacular displays of shape and colour.

Even more recently plant breeders have begun to use other ways of producing new plants. By treating seeds with chemicals or radiation (such as X-rays or gamma rays), they can cause changes in the chromosomes called mutations. These changes affect the nature of the plant. Most mutations are harmful, but some may result in better plants. Some varieties of wheat have been produced in this way.

---

grown for their flowers.
Bramble (*Rubus*) is a genus of rambling plants that includes blackberries, raspberries, loganberries and wineberries.
Broad bean (*Vicia faba*) is a member of the pea family that has large edible seeds.
Broccoli (a variety of *Brassica oleracea*) is a member of the CABBAGE family grown for its small flower heads. They are eaten together with the leaves.
Brussel sprout (a variety of the genus *Brassica oleracea*) is a member of the cabbage family that has large, dense axillary buds. These are the sprouts that are eaten.

C Cabbages are varieties of *Brassica oleracea*.

Bramble fruit

They have very large terminal buds, which form the main bulk of the plant.
Carrot (*Daucus carota*) is a small biennial herb with a large edible tap root.
Cauliflower (a variety of *Brassica oleracea*) is a member of the cabbage family grown for its large white flower head, which is picked and eaten before it comes fully into bloom.
Cherry is a number of trees belonging to the genus *Prunus*. The red or purple fruits are edible drupes. The sweet cherry (*P. avium*) is the main source of fruit. Its wood is used in veneers.
Coffee plant (*Coffea*) is a genus of small trees that are grown for their seeds. The fruits (berries) of the coffee

Wild cherry

plant are harvested, and the seeds, or beans, are used to make coffee.
Cotton plants (*Gossypium*) are 30 species of shrubs that grow in tropical and sub-tropical regions. They have large yellow, purple or white flowers. The fruits are capsules divided into compartments. Each compartment contains a seed surrounded by fine white fibres. These may be up to 5 cm in length.
Cretan date palm (*Phoenix theophrasti*) is a very rare palm tree found mainly in a single grove in Crete. It is threatened with extinction

Plants and Man 59

Plants for food

All the main parts of plants are represented in our food. From various plants we get seeds, fruits, flowers, stems, leaves and roots that can be eaten.

Edible seeds include those of the cereal crops, and the most important of these are RICE, WHEAT and maize. They are grown in many parts of the world and together they produce more than 750,000 million tonnes of grain each year. Other seeds that we eat include peas, soya beans and almonds. Coffee is made from the beans of the COFFEE PLANT.

A vast number of fruits are grown for food. As well as all the well-known fruits, such as peaches, oranges and blackberries, many of our vegetables are also fruits in the botanical sense. Examples of these include tomatoes, cucumbers and MARROWS.

Many flowers, too, are good to eat, although they are usually not allowed to bloom before they are picked. Cauliflowers, various kinds of broccoli and globe artichokes are all flowers.

The stems that we eat include not only above-ground stems but also tubers – modified underground stems. Asparagus, rhubarb and seakale are popular edible stems that grow above the ground. The stems of sugar cane provide 65 per cent of the world's sugar supply. Cultivated tubers include potatoes, Jerusalem ARTICHOKES and yams.

Many plants are eaten for their leaves. The most obvious of these include cabbages, lettuces and leeks. ONIONS are bulbs and consist mostly of

Above: All the parts of a plant are represented in the foods we eat. The edible seeds, fruits, flowers, stems, leaves and roots of various plants are shown here.

---

through damage by tourists.
Cucumber, see MARROW FAMILY.
Cyclamen is a genus of 16 small garden and indoor plants related to the primrose. They come from the Mediterranean region and grow from corms.

D Date palm (*Phoenix dactylifera*) is a tall palm tree, about 25 metres high, that produces large numbers of single-seeded berries. It grows in dry sub-tropical regions.
Dracaena ombet is a palm-like tree that grows in Ethiopia and the Sudan near the Red Sea. It used to be common, but is now becoming rare. The local people use the trunks for firewood and the leaves for basket-weaving.

E Ebony (*Diospyros*) is a genus of trees that have black, heavy heartwood. They are found in tropical and sub-tropical regions. The best wood is obtained from the Ceylon ebony (*D. ebenum*).
Echium is a genus of plants found in the laurel forests of the Canary Islands. They are becoming rare, and this is partly due to the destruction of the forests by farmers.

F Flax (*Linum usitatissimum*) is a herbaceous

Cotton

plant cultivated for the fibres in its stem, in cool climates such as Europe, Russia and North America. The highest yield of fibre is obtained from plants harvested after the seed pods have ripened.
Freesia is a genus of greenhouse plants with trumpet-shaped flowers. They range widely in colour, and these plants can be grown from seeds or corms.

G Gentian (*Gentiana*) is a genus of perennial garden plants with blue or white flowers.
Gladiolus is a genus of monocotyledonous garden plants grown from corms. The flowers are borne on a long spike, and those at the bottom of the spike open first.
Gooseberry (*Ribes grossularia*) is a shrub grown for its green hairy fruits (berries). Currants also belong to the genus *Ribes*.
Grapefruit (*Citrus paradisi*) is a tree that grows about 10 metres tall. It has yellow-skinned fruits (berries) that grow in clusters.

H Hemp (*Cannabis sativa*) is the plant from which

Plants and Man

Below: Honduras mahogany comes from one of the most important timber trees of tropical America. It is used in cabinet-making.

Below: Ebony is a very hard wood. Ebony heartwood is especially valued for making inlays in cabinet work and for piano keys.

Below: Walnut is a tough wood with a particularly attractive grain. It is used to make fine furniture and interior panelling.

Below: Redwood wears well and is thus a useful wood for making garden furniture and siding for homes. It is also used for cabinet work.

Below: Rosewood is a fine reddish wood that takes a high polish. It is used in making furniture and veneers.

Below: Oak is a hard, heavy wood that wears well. It is used in the construction of homes and ships, and in making furniture.

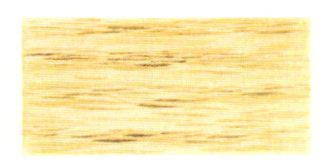

Below: Cherry wood, grown in many parts of the Northern Hemisphere, is an attractive golden-brown wood used to make high-quality veneers.

Below: Balsa wood, grown in tropical areas, is light and buoyant. It is used to make canoes, life-saving apparatus, and model aeroplanes.

Right: Opium poppies (*Papaver somniferum*) are grown in many parts of the world, especially in China, India and the Near East and Mediterranean area. About 2 weeks after the petals fall off, the poppy capsules are harvested for their opium, which is a white, milky juice.

fleshy leaves. TEA is made from the leaves of a small tree.

Since man first discovered edible roots, many more plants of this kind have been produced. When settlers moved to new countries they took their crops with them. Root crops in particular were transported, because they are high yielding crops that are easily grown. As a result they are now found thousands of kilometres from where they first originated. Examples of widely-grown root crops are radishes, carrots, beetroots, and sugar beet.

Plants for materials and chemicals

For thousands of years, plants have provided man with many useful materials in addition to food. Shelter was the next most important need, and the earliest houses were built from mud and grass. Even today, the common reed is still used to thatch the roofs of some houses in Britain. Later, when man had developed the appropriate tools, he used wood to build more solid houses. Today, few houses are built entirely of timber but wood is still used in construction and in making furniture.

There are two main types of timber. Softwoods are conifers, such as pine, spruce, and cedar. Hardwoods are broad-leaved trees, such as beech, oak, and WALNUT. The hardest woods of all are mahogany, TEAK, ROSEWOOD, and EBONY.

After a tree has been felled and cut into lengths, the wood is left to dry out, or season, for about a year. It is then suitable for use. As well as being used in building and furniture, wood is used to make telegraph poles and fencing, and it is also used as a fuel for domestic fires.

---

hemp fibres are obtained. It grows in sub-tropical regions. The drug marijuana is also obtained from this plant.
Hibiscadelphus is a rare Hawaiian plant whose flowers are adapted for pollination by the Hawaiian honey creepers. Due to the destruction of their habitat by man, both the plants and birds are in danger of extinction.
Hydrangea is a genus of 35 species of shrubs and climbing plants. *H. macrophylla* is a common shrub in British gardens. Its flowers may be pink or blue.

J **Jasmine** (*Jasminium*) is a genus of garden shrubs usually grown against walls.
Jute (*Corchorus*) is a genus of 2 species of annual plants related to the lime, mostly found in Bangladesh. The stem fibres are coarser than those of FLAX and HEMP, but they used for making sacking and carpets.

K **Kidney bean** (*Phaseolus vulgaris*) is a member of the pea family. It is also called the French bean. Some varieties are grown for their edible fruits (pods). Others, such as haricot beans, are grown for their seeds only.

L **Lady's slipper orchid** (*Cypridedium calceolus*) is the rarest British plant, known only in one place. It is also becoming rare in the rest of Europe.
Leek, see ONION.
Lemon (*Citrus limon*) is a small tree with yellow fruits (berries). Lemon fruits have less sugar than ORANGES, and thus are more acid to taste.
Lettuce (*Lactuca sativa*). A leafy salad vegetable related to the dandelion and daisy.
Love-in-a-mist (*Nigella damascena*) is an annual garden plant with finely-cut leaves and blue flowers.
Lupin (*Lupinus*) is a genus of about 300 species of herbaceous plants. They are perennials and several are grown as garden plants.

M **Mahogany** (*Swietenia*) is a genus of trees

Gladioli

Hydrangea

Plants and Man 61

Below: Teak is a hard wood when seasoned, and is popular for making veneers and furniture. It is also used in building ships.

Below: Ash, from Europe and North America, is a tough, springy timber used for making the handles of large tools, such as spades.

Below: Beech wood is valued for its hardness and smoothness. It makes good everyday furniture and handles for small tools.

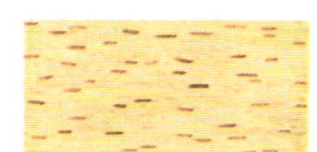

Below: Pine is a popular light-coloured wood for making kitchen furniture and cupboards. It also has many other uses.

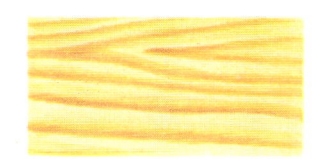

Below: The wood of the Douglas fir is often sold as 'Oregon pine'. The reddish-yellow timber is often used in construction.

Below: The whitish wood from lime trees is soft but firm and it is used for carving. Lime trees are grown all over the Northern Hemisphere.

Below: Wood from spruces, which are conifers from the cooler regions of the Northern Hemisphere, is used for indoor woodwork, boxes, matches and paper.

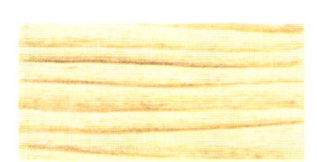

Below: Yew is an increasingly popular, yellow-orange wood used in fine reproduction furniture, usually as a veneer.

Below: The wood of cedar trees is used for making cigar boxes, bottom planking in yachts and for lining clothing storage cupboards.

Much of the softwood that is felled is made into paper. In this process the wood is first turned into pulp, which is done either chemically or by a machine. The pulp is refined by beating, which makes the fibres frayed and flexible. The grade of paper depends on this stage. Fibres beaten for a long time will produce the finest grades. Coarse papers, such as newspaper, do not need any further treatment. But the paper used in this book has been through several treatments to achieve this quality. Other kinds of treatment are used to produce grease-proof paper, cardboard, blotting-paper, tissues, and even paper clothes!

Wood is not the only product obtained from trees. Various species give us other materials essential to modern life. The bark of cork oaks is stripped off at intervals to give us cork – familiar to us as the stoppers of wine bottles. The RUBBER TREE is tapped for its milky white sap, called latex. This is treated by an industrial process to give us rubber. The saps of other trees supply us with natural resins and gums, such as resin from pine trees and canada balsam from the silver fir. Carnauba wax is obtained from the leaves of the carnauba palm. The waxy layer on the outside of the leaves is beaten off and is used in making polishes, crayons, cosmetics and carbon paper.

In addition to paper, other everyday materials are made from plant fibres. HEMP consists of fibres from the stem of the hemp plant. It is made into rope. The fibres of the sisal plant are also made into rope and string. Flax plants produce finer fibres that are used to make linen. Cotton, the finest of all the plant fibres, is obtained from the seed pods of the COTTON PLANT.

Some drugs and poisons are obtained from plants. The foxglove contains the poison digitalin. However, this can be used, in very small quantities, to treat some forms of heart disease as it makes the heart beat faster. Opium is a

Above: Rubber trees are tapped every few days by making a deep, sloping cut round the bark. The white, milky latex then seeps out until the wound heals. The latex is taken to a processing plant where it is turned into rubber by treating it with chemicals.

---

found in wet tropical forests. The 2 most important trees are the West Indian mahogany (*S. mahagoni*) and the Honduras mahogany (*S. macrophylla*).
Maize (*Zea mais*) is an annual grain crop principally grown in tropical and sub-tropical regions, but also grown in some temperate areas. There are a number of types, including dent corn, pop corn and flint corn.
Marrow family. Marrows, courgettes, squashes and pumpkins are all fruits (berries) of the genus *Cucurbita*. Many varieties are grown all over the world. Water melons (*Citrullus vulgaris*) are grown in many warm temperate, sub-tropical and tropical regions. Cucumbers and other melons are fruits of the genus *Cucumis*.

O **Oats** (*Avena sativa*) are grown as a grain crop in temperate regions. They can easily be distinguished from other grain crops by their spreading flower head with hanging spikelets — quite unlike the tight flower heads of wheat, rye and barley.
Onion (*Allium cepa*) is a vegetable widely grown from a bulb, particularly in Egypt, Europe and north America. There are a number of varieties grown for cooking, pickling or eating raw in salads. Leeks, garlic and chives also belong to the genus *Allium*.
Orange. Several varieties of tree bear orange fruits (berries), including sweet oranges (*Citrus sinensis*) and Seville oranges (*C. aurantium*).

P **Pea** (*Pisum sativum*) is an annual plant grown for the seeds contained in its pods.
Peach (*Prunus persica*) is a small willowy deciduous tree that bears velvety-skinned fruits (drupes).
Pears include a variety of trees all descended from the common pear (*Pyrus communis*), a tree that grows wild all over Europe. The fruits (pomes) are formed in

Oats

Hemp

Plants and Man

[Illustrations of indoor plants: Swiss cheese plant, Orange tree, Rubber plant, Poinsettia, Christmas cactus, Alpine violet, Ivy, Busy Lizzie, Lady's pocket book, Begonia Rex, Mexican sunball, Tradescantia]

dangerous drug obtained from the unripe seed capsules of the opium poppy. It can be used to make codeine, which is a mild pain-killer, or morphine and pethidine, which are powerful pain-killers. Cocaine is a drug that acts like an anaesthetic. It is obtained from the cocoa plant. Quinine is extracted from the bark of the cinchona tree. This drug was once used to treat malaria, but it has now been replaced by other drugs. Caffeine is a drug, found in tea and coffee, that acts as a stimulant. The leaves of the tobacco plant contain nicotine, which is another drug that stimulates the nervous system.

The deadly poisons found in plants include atropine from deadly nightshade, and coniine from hemlock. Curare is a mixture of deadly drugs. In the forests of South America it is used to tip blow-gun darts and arrows for hunting.

Above: There are many varied indoor plants. Some are grown for their attractive foliage, others for their showy flowers or fruits, and some just for their unusual appearance.

Plants for pleasure

As civilizations grew, people had time to relax and enjoy the things around them. Nature has her own beauty, but for thousands of years man has delighted in using flowers to create beautiful gardens.

The Bible tells us of the Hanging Gardens of Babylon, which the Greeks described as one of the seven wonders of the world. Since then gardens have reflected the tastes of society. The ruins of Pompeii show us the small enclosed gardens of the Romans. Much later, in the 1600s, the gardens of the great European houses and palaces were extremely formal, and were laid out with great care. In the 1700s there was a reaction to this formal style, and men such as Capability Brown changed gardens into 'natural' landscapes.

---

the same way as APPLES.
Plums include a number of fruits (drupes) of trees belonging to the genus *Prunus*. Also in this group are damsons, gages, sloes, and bullace.
Potato (*Solanum tuberosum*) is a plant of the nightshade family grown for its tubers. It is one of the most important food plants of the world, and there are several varieties.
Radish (*Raphanus sativus*) is a widely grown root crop used in salads.
Rhubarb (*Rheum rhaponticum*) is a perennial plant grown for its leaf stalks. The leaves are not eaten as they contain oxalic acid poison.
Rice (*Oryza sativa*) is the

Rice harvest in Guyana

chief cereal crop of Asia, developed from a marsh plant and adapted to growing in flooded areas. Rice seed is sown in nurseries and the seedlings later transplanted into flooded fields. A few weeks before harvesting the fields are drained to allow the ears to dry off and the grain to ripen.
Roses (*Rosa*) are probably the most popular of all garden plants. There are several types, including bush, shrub, standard, rambling, climbing and miniature roses. Breeders are constantly trying to produce new varieties with ever more beautiful blooms.
Rosewood (*Dalbergia*) is a genus of evergreen trees that grow about 10 metres

Sugar cane harvest

tall. They all have attractive wood, and the most important species are the Brazilian rosewood (*D. nigra*), the Honduras rosewood (*D. stevensonii*), the Indian sissoo (*D. sissoo*) and the East Indian rosewood (*D. latifolia*).
Rubber tree (*Hevea braziliensis*) is a tree that is more accurately called the Pará rubber to distinguish it from the rubber tree (*Ficus elastica*), an Asian tree commonly grown as a houseplant. The Pará rubber comes from Brazil, but most rubber plantations are now

Plants and Man 63

Bottom right: Roses are one of the most popular garden plants. They have beautiful flowers, which are often sweet-smelling. Rose breeders spend much time in establishing new varieties, and roses are grown in several forms.

Right: Some gardens are very formal. This style of garden is popular in Japan, where such settings are used for quiet relaxation and contemplation.

In the past gardening was largely a rich man's pastime, but today nearly everybody has a garden of some kind. It may be a large country garden or a small patch at the back of a town house. The style may be formal, informal or a mixture of both, and gardens now reflect the tastes of their individual owners. The wide range of plants and garden materials now available make it possible to create any style of garden desired.

All the garden flowers, shrubs and trees are descended from wild plants. Careful selection and breeding, including hybridization, has being going on for over 3,000 years, since the Egyptian and Assyrian civilizations. The skills required to tend and cultivate plants were passed on to the Greeks and Romans. During the Dark Ages, monks used these skills to cultivate garden plants in the privacy of their cloisters. At the same time the Chinese and Japanese gardeners were developing their own gardening techniques, and plants were also being cultivated in Central and South America. Modern gardens contain plants from all over the world, and we owe this to the great European explorers of the 1400s to 1800s who brought back unknown seeds, bulbs and living plants from their voyages. Some of these did not survive in their new surroundings, but many of them have become successful and popular garden plants. For example, chrysanthemums originated in Japan, pelargoniums and gladioli came from South America, and hyacinths were first bred in Asia. Subsequent breeding and selection has produced all the different varieties of these plants that we know today.

Plants in danger

The number of animals that are threatened with extinction is increasing, and there is much worldwide concern about this. However, because

---

found in Malaysia.
Runner bean (*Phaseolus coccineus*) is a climbing plant of the pea family, also known as the scarlet runner,

Young teak trees

that is grown for its fruits (pods).
Rye (*Secale cereale*) is an important grain crop in the colder regions of Russia and Europe. It is used for making bread, gin and beer, and the young shoots are sometimes fed to animals.
Seakale (*Crambe maritima*) is a seaside plant related to the wallflower. If it is grown in the dark, its leaf stalks remain white and can be eaten as a vegetable.
Sisal (*Agave sisilana*) is a succulent plant related to the American century plant. It

contains tough fibres in its leaves that are extracted and used to make rope and string.
Soya (*Glycine max*) is an annual plant of the pea family grown for its seeds. Soya beans are used to make an edible oil, or they can be eaten as a vegetable. Soya beans contain a high proportion of protein and are therefore a useful source of food.
Strawberry (*Fragaria*) is a number of cultivated and wild plants, mostly grown in Europe and America. The juicy, red edible structures

are in fact false fruits, because they are formed from swollen receptacles. The true fruits of the strawberry are the achenes on the out-

Tea plant

side of the edible part.
Sugar beet (*Beta vulgaris*, sub-species *cicla*) is a root crop closely related to the BEETROOT. It is grown in Europe, North America and Russia, and is an important source of sugar in countries too cold to grow sugar cane.
Sugar cane (*Saccharum officinarum*) is a grass whose stems, or canes, contain a large amount of sugar. It is grown in tropical regions, where it gives the best sugar yield, and in sub-tropical areas.
Sweet pea (*Lathyrus odoratus*) is an annual

Plants and Man

Above: The lady's slipper orchid (*Cypripedium calceolus*) is the rarest plant in Britain, and is becoming rare all over the Northern Hemisphere.

Right: The silver sword (*Argyroxiphium macrocephalum*) is only found on a crater of the volcanic Maui Island – one of the Hawaiian Islands.

it is less easy to feel sympathy for a plant, we hear much less about the plants that are also becoming rare. In fact about 25,000 species of plants (ten per cent of the world's flora) are nearly extinct.

We should be concerned about this because animals and man depend on plants for survival. If areas of plant life are destroyed, then the animals that live in those areas will die out. At the same time many plants that might be useful to man are also being destroyed. This is particularly true of the tropical rain forests. When areas of these forests are cut for timber or cleared for agriculture, the plant and animal populations are reduced in numbers. Some localized plants are wiped out altogether. In the Phillipines, 172,000 hectares of forest are being removed every year. In the Amazon basin land is being cleared for development. In this relatively unexplored area we are probably losing many species of plants before they have even been discovered. Some of those plants could, perhaps, have provided us with new sources of food, new drugs or new materials, such as oils.

This could be described as one of the penalties of progress but many people believe that the land is actually unsuitable for grazing or growing crops. In addition, removing forests from hilly areas increases the chance of soil erosion, which leaves the land bare and useless.

Plants are also being threatened by the activities of man in many other areas of the world. Overgrazing dry areas has led to the formation of deserts, such as the belt from the Sahel in Africa to south-western Asia. Goats in particular are responsible for such effects, as they eat anything green, including young tree shoots.

Many of the world's islands have also suffered. On Hawaii there are 800 endangered species of plants, and 273 are listed as extinct. St Helena in the South Atlantic has been affected by both grazing animals and plants introduced from outside. Goats, first introduced in 1513, devastated the forests within 100 years. In 1805 a botanical expedition discovered 31 species of native plants. Eleven of those are now extinct. The goats are now under control, but two introduced plants, New Zealand flax and gorse, are causing more problems. They are spreading over the island, swamping the natural flora.

---

climbing plant that produces a great show of sweet smelling flowers.
Syagrus sancona is an endangered species of palm tree that grows in the rain forests of Columbia. Areas of this rain forest are now being cleared for grazing.

T **Teak** (*Tectona grandis*) is a large tree that grows in India and Burma. Its heartwood is golden yellow after the tree has been cut, but becomes brown and mottled when seasoned.
Tea plant (*Camellia sinensis*) is a small tree grown in tropical and sub-tropical areas of the world. Tea is made from its leaves, and the finest tea is made by using only young shoots.

Walnuts

Tobacco plant (*Nicotiana tabacum*) is an annual plant belonging to the nightshade family. It is grown in many parts of the world, and its leaves are harvested and cured to make tobacco.
Tomato (*Lycopersicon esculentum*) is an annual plant belonging to the nightshade family grown for its red or orange fruits (berries).

W **Wahlenbergia linifolia** is a small shrub with white bell-shaped flowers that grows on the island of St Helena. Because it is small it is in danger of being swamped by the plants that have been introduced to the island by man.
Wallflower (*Cheiranthus*) is a genus of popular biennial

Yams

garden plants.
Walnut (*Juglans*) is a genus of 17 species of deciduous trees. The best nuts (seeds) are obtained from the fruits (drupes) of the English walnut (*J. regia*).
Wheat (*Triticum*). Several species of this grain crop are grown in Europe, Russia, Asia, America, and Australia. It is used for making flour for bread, biscuits and pasta.

Y **Yam** (*Dioscorea*) is a genus of climbing plants grown for their edible tubers in America, Asia and Africa.

Index

66 Index

Page numbers in **bold** type refer to the reference sections. Page numbers in *italics* refer to illustrations.

A

- Acacia, **36**, *36*
- Achenes, **36**
- Adaptation in plants, 49-55
- Adder's tongue, *see* Ophioglossum
- Adder's tongue spearwort, **57**
- Adiantum, **30**
- Agaricus, **21**, 25
- Alder, **36**, 38
- Algae, 3, **3**
  - Antherozoid, **17**, 20
  - Bacteria and, 17–20
  - Blue-green, *5*, 18
  - *Ceratium*, 18
  - *Chara*, 19
  - Characteristics, 18
  - *Chlamydomonas*, **17**, 19, *20*
  - Cladophora, *18*, 19
  - Colony, 19, *19*
  - Cyanophytes, **17**
  - Diatoms, *3*, *17*, 18–19, **18**
  - *Euglena*, **18**, *18*, 19
  - Euglenophytes, **18**
  - Evolution, 4, *5*
  - Fucus, **18**, *18*
  - Fungi and, 25, 53
  - Kelp, 20
  - Lichens, 25
  - *Nostoc*, *18*
  - Oogonium, **19**, *19*, 20
  - Pigments, 16
  - Plankton, 18
  - *Pleurococcus*, 18, **19**, *19*
  - Pyrrophytes, **19**
  - Reproduction, 20, *20*
  - Rhodophytes, **19**, 20
  - *Spirogyra*, 19, **20**, *20*, *50*
  - *Stigeoclonium*, 19, **20**
  - Stoneworts, 19, **20**
  - Ulothrix, 19, **20**
  - Volvox, 19, *19*, **20**
  - Xanthophytes, **20**
  - Zoospores, 20
  - Zygote, 20
- Almond, **57**, 59
- Alpine
  - Violet, *62*
  - Zones, **6**, *6*, **49**
- *Amanita*, **21**, *23–24*, 25
- *Amaryllis* family, **36**
- Amazonian water lily, **49**, *49*, 50
- American
  - Century plant, **49**, 52
  - Resurrection plant, **49**, 52
- Amino acids, **8**, 15
- Anabolism, **8**
- Anemone, **36**
- Angiosperms, **3**, 6, 33, 36
  - *See also* Flowering plants
- Annuals, **36**
- Annulus, **21**, 24
  - Moss, **26**
  - Toadstool, **21**, *24*
- Anisogamy, **17**
- Anther, 37, *39*
- Antheridium, **17**, *17*
- Antherozoid, 20
- Anthocyanin, 16, *16*
- Antirrhinum, *15*, **36**
- Apple moss, *29*
- Aquatic plants, 49–50, *49–50*
- Archegonium, **26**, *26*, 29, *29*
- Arthrophytes, **30**
- Artichoke, **57**, 59, *59*
- Ascomycetes, **21**, 22, *22*, 25
- Ascus, **21**, 22
- Asexual reproduction, **17**
  - *See also* Reproduction
- Ash, **36**, *36*, 41, *61*
- Asparagus, **57**, 59, *59*
- *Asplenium*, **30**, 31
- Aster, **57**
- Atropine, 62
- Aubergine, **57**, *57*
- Aubretia, **57**
- Azolla, 31, **49**, *51*

B

- Bacillariophytes, *see* Diatoms
- Bacteria, **17**, *17*
  - Algae and, 17–20
  - Blue-green algae and, 18
  - Characteristics, 17
  - Culture, *18*
  - Effects of, 17
  - Forms, *17*
  - Nitrogen-fixing, 15, 17, **19**
  - Photosynthesis by, 17
  - Plants and, 15, 17
  - Putrefaction by, 17, **19**
  - Uses of, 17, *17–18*
- Banana, **57**, *58*
- Banyan, **49**, *54*
- Bark, 45–46
- Barley, **57**
- Barrel cactus, *52*
- Basidiomycetes, **21**, 22–25
- Basidium, **21**, 22
- Beech, **36**, 60, *61*
- Bee orchid, **37**, *39*
- Beetroot, **57**, *59*, 60
- Begonia, 47, **57**, *62*
- Bennettitales, **3**, *5*, 6
- Berries, **37**
- Biennials, **37**
- Bindweeds, **37**, *37*, 55
- Biome, **3**, 6
- Birch, **37**
- Bird of paradise flower, *36*
- Bird's nest orchid, **49**, *50*
- Bishop's mitre, *52*
- Bladderworts, **50**, 56
- Bluebell, *see* Hyacinth
- Blue-green algae, 25
- Blusher, *21*
- Bog moss, **26**
- Boletus, **21**, *24*
- Botany, **3**
- *Botrychium*, **30**
- Bracket fungi, 23–24, *23*
- Bracken, *32*
  - *See also Pteridium*
- Bramble, 55, **58**, 58
- Bristlecone pine, *4*
- Broad bean, 43, *43*, **58**
- Broccoli, **58**, *59*
- Bromeliads, **50**, 55, *55*
- Broomrapes, **50**, 55
- Brussel sprout, **58**
- Bryophytes, **3**, **26**
- *Bryum*, **26**, *28*
- Bulbs, 46, *46*, 57
- Burdock, *41*
- Busy Lizzie, *62*
- Buttercup, **37**, *37*
- Butterworts, **50**, 56

C

- Cabbage, **58**, *59*
- Cactus, 36, *46*, **50**, *51*, 52–3, *52–3*
- Calamites, 4, 30
- Californian
  - Poppy, **50**
  - Redwood, *3*
- *Calypogeia*, 26, **26**, *27*
- Calyptra, **26**
- Calyx, **37**
- Cambium, 45
- Cambrian period, **3**
- Campions, **37**
- Canadian pond weed, **50**
- Candle plant, **51**, 53
- Capsule, **37**
  - Moss, *27*
- Carbohydrate, **8**, 14
- Carbon cycle, *15*
- Carboniferous period, **3**, 4
- Carnauba palm, 61
- Carnivorous plants, 55–6, *55–6*
- Carotenes, 16, *16*
- Carpel, 37, *38*
- Carrot, **58**, *59*, 60
- Catabolism, **8**
- Catkins, 38, *39*
- Cauliflower, **58**, *59*
- Cedar, 33, **33**, *33*, 60, *61*
- Celeriac, *59*
- Cell, plant, **8**, *8*
  - Differentiation, 9–10
  - Division, 10–11, *10–11*
  - Structure, 8–9, *8*
- Cell wall, **8**, *8–9*
- Cellulose, **8**, 9, *9*
- *Ceratium*, 18
- Cereals, *58*, 59
- *Ceterach officinarum*, *30*
- *Chamaecereus silvestrii*, *52*
- Chanterelle, **22**, *24*
- *Chara*, 19
- Cheese, 17, *17*
- Cherry, **58**, *59*
- Chipboard, 34
- *Chlamydomonas*, **17**, 19, *20*
- Chlorophyll, 13, *14*, 16
- Chloroplast, *8*, **9**, 13
- Chlorosis, **9**
- Cholla, *52*
- Christmas cactus, *62*
- Chromatin, **9**
- Chromoplast, *8*, **9**
- Chromosome, 8, **9**, 11
- Chrysanthemum, *8*, 47
- Chrysophytes, **17**
- *Cladonia*, *23*
- *Cladophora*, 19
- Class, **3**
- Classification, **3**
- Clematis, **38**
- Climax, *see* Succession
- Clover, *37*, **38**
- Clubmosses, 4, *5*, 30, *31*
  - *See also Lycopodium*
  - *Selaginella*, **32**
- Cocaine, 62
- Cocoa, *58*, 62
- Coconut, *36*, 42, *43*
- Codeine, 62
- Coffee, **58**, *58*, 59, 62
- Collenchyma, 9, **9**
- Colour, plants, 15–6
- Columella, **26**
- Cones, 33, *33*, 35
- Conifer, **3**, *5*, 6, 33–4, *34*
- Coniine, 62
- Coprinus, **22**
- Cordaitales, **3**, 4, *4–5*, 6
- Cork, *9*, 10, 45
- Corm, 46, *46*
- Corolla, **38**
- Cotton plant, **58**, *59*, 61
- Cotyledon, 36, **38**
- Cow parsley, **38**
- Creosote bush, **51**, 52, *53*
- Cretaceous period, **4**, 6
- Cretan date palm, **58**
- Crocus, **38**, *38*, 46, *46*, 48
- Crops, *58*, 59–60
- Cucumber, 42, 59
  - *See also* Marrow family
- Curare, 62
- Cutin, 74, **74**
- Cyanophytes, **17**
- Cycads, **4**, *5*, 6, 33, **33**, *33*
- Cyclamen, **59**
- Cypresses, 33, **33**, *34*
- Cytoplasm, 8, *8*, **10**

D

- Daffodil, *16*, **38**, 46, *46*
- Daisy, **38**, *38*, 48
- Dandelion, **38**, 41, *41*
- Date palm, *58*, **59**
- Dawn redwood, **33**
- Deadly nightshade, *39*, 62
  - *See also* Nightshade family
- Deadnettle, *see* Nettle
- Death cap, **24**
  - *See also Amanita*,
- De Candolle, Augustin, **4**
- Decay, *see* Putrefaction, **19**
- Deciduous
  - Forest, *6*
  - Tree, **39**
- Dehiscent fruit, **39**
- Deoxyribonucleic acid (DNA), 8, **10**
- Desert, **51**
  - Plants, 51–3, *51–3*
- Devonian period, 4, **4**
- Diatoms, *3*, *17*, 18, **18**, 19
- Dicotyledons, 36, *37*
- Dioecious plant, **39**
- Division, **4**
- DNA, 8, **10**
- Dodder, **51**, 54–5, *54*
- Dog rose, *37*
- Dogwood, **39**
- Douglas fir, **33**, *34*, *61*
- *Dracaena ombet*, **59**
- Drupe, **39**
- Dryad's saddle fungus, *23*
- *Dryopteris*, **30**
- Dry rot, **22**
- Duckweed, 50, *50*, **51**

E

- Ebony, **59**, 60, *60*
- Echium, **59**
- Ecology, **4**
- Eelgrass, **51**
- Elater, **26**
- Elaterophore, **27**
- Elder, **39**, *39*
- Elm, **39**
- Endangered species, plants, 63–4, *64*
- Endoplasmic reticulum, 8, *8*, **10**
- Endospermic seed, **39**, 40, *43*
- Environment, **4**
  - Plants, 6–7, 43–55
- Enzyme, 8, **10**, 11, 12–3
- Ephedra, 6, 33, **33**
- Ephemeral plants, **51**, *51*, 52
- Epidermis, 10, **10**
- Epigeal germination, **39**, *43*
- Epiphytes, **51**, 55, *55*
- Epyphytic fern, *32*
- *Equisetum*, 30, *30*
- Ergot of rye, 22, **22**
- Eucalyptus, **40**
- *Euglena*, **18**, 19
- Euglenophytes, **18**
- Evergreen, **40**
- Evergreen trees, **33**
- Evolution,
  - Living fossils, *99*
  - Plants, 68–70, *69*
- Excretion, **4**

F

- Fairy ring champignon, **22**
- False acacia, *11*
- Family, **4**
- Fats and oils, **10**
- Fermentation, 22
- Ferns, **4**, 30–2
  - *Adiantum*, **30**
  - *Asplenium*, **30**, 31
  - *Botrychium*, **30**, *32*
  - *Dryopteris*, **30**
  - Evolution, 4, *5*, 30
  - Gametophyte, **29**, 31, *32*
  - Life-cycle, *32*
  - *Marsilea*, **31**
  - *Ophioglossum*, **31**
  - *Osmunda*, **31**
  - *Phyllitis*, **31**, *32*
  - Prothallus, **31**, 32, *32*
  - *Psilotum*, 30, **31**, *31*
  - *Pteridium*, **32**, *32*
  - Reproduction, 31–2, *32*
  - Royal, *30*
  - Sorus, *31*, 32, **32**, *32*
  - Sporangium, 31, **32**, *32*
  - Sporophyte, **29**, 31, *32*
  - *Tmesipteris*, 30, **32**
  - Tree, *31*
- Fertilization, **18**
  - *See also* Reproduction
- Filicophytes, **30**
- Firs, 33, **33**, *34*
- Flagellum, **18**
- Flax, **59**, 61
- Flowering ash, *36*
- Flowering plants, 36–48
  - Bacteria and, 15, 17
  - Bulbs, 46, *46*
  - Corm, 46, *46*
  - Cotyledon, 36, **38**
  - Dicotyledons, 36, *37*
  - Evolution, *5*
  - Fruit, 40–2, *41*
  - Grafting, 47–8
  - Leaf, 11, *12*, 37
  - Monocotyledons, 36
  - Movement, *47*, 48, *48*
  - Pollination, 38–40, *39–40*
  - Propagation, 46–8
  - Reproduction, 37–44, 46–8
  - Rhizomes, 46, *46*
  - Roots, 44–5, *44–5*
  - Runners, 46, *46*
  - Seed, 40–4
  - Smallest, 50, **56**
  - Stem, 11, *12*, 37, *38*, 44, *44*
  - Structure, 36–7
  - Tendrils, *47*, 48
- Fly agaric, *see Amanita*
- Follicle, **40**
- *Fontinalis*, **27**
- Food poisoning, **18**
- Forest
  - Deciduous, *6*
  - Rain, 6–7, *7*
  - Temperate, 7
- Forget-me-not, **40**
- Formation, **4**, 6
- Forsythia, **40**
- Fossils, living, *35*
- Foxglove, 38, **40**, *40*, 61
- Freesia, **59**
- Fruit
  - Capsule, **37**
  - Dehiscent, **39**
  - Dispersal, 41–2, *41*
  - Indehiscent, **42**
  - Structure, 40–1, *41*
- Fuchsia, **40**
- *Fucus*, **18**
- *Funaria*, **27**
- Fungi, **5**, 21–4
  - Algae and, 25, 53
  - Ascomycetes, **21**, 22, *22*, 25
  - Ascus, **21**, 22
  - Basidiomycetes, **21**, 22–5
  - Bracket, 23–4, *23*
  - Conidia, 22
  - Evolution, *5*
  - Hyphae, 21, *21*
  - Mushrooms, 22, **23**, *24*
  - Mycelium, 21–3, 25
  - Phycomycetes, 21–2, **24**
  - Reproduction, 21, *21*, 22–3
  - Rust, 21–2, *22*
  - Sporangia, 21, *21*
  - Toadstools, 22–5, *23–4*, **25**
  - Zygospore, 21

G

- Gametes, **18**
- Gametophyte, **27**
  - Fern, 31, *32*
  - Liverwort, 29, *29*
  - Moss, 29, *29*
- Gardens, 62–3, *63*
- Gentian, **59**
- Genus, **5**
- Geranium, **40**, *40*, 42, 47
- Germination, 42–4, *43*
  - Epigeal, **39**
  - Hypogeal, **42**
- Giant
  - Puff balls, **22**, 23, *24*
  - Redwood, **34**, *34*
- Ginger, *59*
- Ginkgos, **5**, *5*, 6, *35*
- Gladiolus, **59**, *60*
- Glasswort, 51, **51**, *51*
- Gnetales, **5**, *5*, *6*, 33
- Gnetum, 6, 33, **34**
- Golgi apparatus, *8*, 9, **11**
- Good-luck plant, 46
- Gooseberry, 47, **59**, *59*
- Gorse, **40**
- Grafting, 47–8
- Grapefruit, **59**
- Grasses, *37*, 38, **41**, 57
- Grassland, 7
- Groundsel, **41**
- Gymnosperms, **5**, 33–5
  - Life-cycle, *35*
  - Reproduction, 34–5, *35*

H

- Habitat, **5**
  - *See also* Environment
- Halophytes, 50–1, **51**, *51*
- Hart's tongue, *32*
  - *See also Phyllitis*
- Hazel, 38, **41**, *42*
- Heartwood, **42**
- *Helvella lacunosa*, *22*
- Hemlock
  - Conifer, **34**
  - Herbaceous, **41**
- Hemp, **59**, 61
- Hepaticae, **27**
- Herbaceous plants, **41**
- Hibiscadelphus, **60**
- Holly, **41**
- Hollyhock, **41**
- Honey fungus, **23**, *23*
- Honeysuckle, **41**, *41*, 55
- Hooke, Robert, **5**
- Hooker, Joseph, **5**
- Hornbeam, **42**
- Horse chestnut, *41*, **42**
- Horsetail, 4, *5*, 30, *31*
  - *See also Equisetum*
- Hyacinths, **42**
- Hybrids, 58
- Hydrangea, **60**, *60*
- Hydrophytes, 49–50, *49–50*, **52**
- Hyphae 21, *21*
- *Hypnum cupressiforme*, **27**, *28*
- Hypogeal germination, **42**, *42*

I

- Indehiscent fruit, **42**
- Indusium, *see* Sorus, **32**
- Ink cap, *24–5*
  - *See also Coprinus*
- Insects, pollination by, 38–9, *39*
- Involucre, **27**
- Iris, *36*, **42**, 46, *46*
- *Isoetes*, 30, **30**, *31*
- Isogamy, **18**
- Ivy, **42**, *42*, 55, *62*

J

- Jacaranda, **42**
- Jasmine, **61**
- Jew's ear fungus, 23, **23**
- Joshua tree, *52*
- Judas tree, **42**
- Jungle, *see* Tropical forest
- Junipers, **34**, *34*
- Jurassic period, **5**
- Jute, **60**, *61*

K

- Kelp, 20
- Kidney bean, **60**
- Kingdom, **5**

L

- Laburnum, *41*, 42, *42*, **43**
- Lady's pocket book, *62*
- Lady's slipper orchid, **60**, *64*
- Laminaria, *18*, **19**
- Larches, 33, **34**, *34*
- Laurel family, **43**, *43*
- Leaf, 11, *12*, 37
- Legume, **43**, 57
- Lemon, *59*, **60**
- Lepidodendron, 4, 30
- Lesser bindweed, *37*
- Lettuce, **60**
- *Leucobryum glaucum*, *28*
- Lianas, *7*, **52**
- Lichens, **23**, 25, *25*
- Lignin, 10, **11**
- Lily, **43**
- Lily of the valley, **43**, *43*
- Lime, **43**, *61*
- Linnaeus, Carolus, **5**
- Liverworts
  - Archegonium, **26**, *26*, 29, *29*
  - *Calypogeia*, **26**, *27*
  - Calyptra, **26**
  - Elater, **26**
  - Elaterophore, **27**
  - Evolution, *5*
  - Gametophyte, **27**, 29, *29*
  - Involucre, **27**
  - *Lophocolea*, **27**, *27*
  - *Marchantia*, 26, **27**, *27*, 28
  - *Pellia*, 26, *27*, **28**
  - Reproduction, 28–9, *29*
  - *Riccardia*, 27, **29**
  - Sporogonium, 29, **29**, *29*
  - Sporophyte, 29, **29**
  - Thallus, 26, 29, **29**
- Living fossil, *35*
- Loosestrife, 39, **43**
- *Lophocolea*, 26, **27**, *27*
- Lords-and-ladies, 39–40, *40*, **43**
- Love-in-a-mist, **60**
- *Lunularia cruciata*, *29*
- Lupin, *47*, **60**
- Lycophytes, 4, **6**, 30, **31**
- *Lycopodium*, *30*, **31**

M

- Magnolia, **44**
- Mahogany, 60, **60**, *60*
- Maidenhair fern, *see Adiantum*
- Maidenhair tree, 33, **33**, *35*
- Maize, **61**
  - Food, as, 59, *59*
  - Origin, *58*
  - Seed, *43*, 44
  - Selective breeding, *57*, 58
  - Stem, *44*
- Man, plants and, 121-28
- Mangroves, *49*, 50, **52**
- Maple, **44**
- *Marchantia*, 26, **27**, *27*, 28
- Maritime pine, *34*

Index

Marram grass, 50, 52, **52**, *52*
Marrow family, 59, **61**
Marsilea, **31**
Meiosis, 11, **11**, *11*
Mendel, Gregor, **6**
Meristem, 44–5
Mesophyll cells, **11**, *12*
Metabolism, **11**
Mexican sunball, 62
Middle lamella, **11**
Mildew, 21–2
Mimosa, 48, *48*
Mineral salts, **11**, 15
Mistletoe, **52**, *53*, 54, *54*
Mitochondria, 8, *8*, **11**
Mitosis, 10–1, *10*, **12**
Mnium, **28**, *28*
Monkey puzzle tree, *6*, **35**
Monocotyledons, 36
Monoecious plant, **44**
Moonwort, *32*
Morel, 22, *22*, *23*
Morphine, 62
Morphology, **6**
Mosses, 26–9
    Antheridium, *29*
    Archegonium, **26**, *26*, 29, *29*
    Bryum, **26**, *28*
    Calyptra, **26**
    Capsule, *27*
    Columella, **26**
    Environment, 90, *90*, 92, 116
    Evolution, *5*
    Fontinalis, *27*
    Funaria, *27*
    Gametophyte, **27**, *29*
    Involucre, **27**
    Mnium, **28**, *28*
    Operculum, **28**
    Paraphyses, **28**
    Peristome teeth, **28**
    Polytrichum, *27*, **28**
    Reproduction, 28–9, *29*
    Sphagnum, **28**, *28*, **29**
    Spore sac, *29*
    Sporogonium, **29**, *29*, *29*
    Sporophyte, *29*, **29**
Moulds, 85
Mucor, *see* Pin mould
Musci, **28**
Mushrooms, 22, **23**, *24*
Mycelium, 21–3, *25*
Mycorrhiza, 25, 54

N
Nectar, 39
Nettle, **44**
Nicotine, 62
Nitrogen cycle, *15*
Nitrogen-fixing bacteria, 15, 17, **19**
Nightshade family, **44**
Non-endospermic seed, **45**
Nuclear membrane, **12**
Nucleolus, 8, **12**
Nucleus, cell, 8, *8*, **12**
Nut, 42, 45

O
Oak, *44*, **45**, 60, *60*
Oarweed, *19*
Oats, **61**, *61*
Oils and fats, **10**
Old man of the desert, **52**, *52*
Old man's beard, 41, *42*
    See also Clematis
Onion, 59, **61**
Oogamy, **19**
Oogonium, **19**, *19*, 20
Oosphere, *see* Archegonium, **26**, *26*, 29
Operculum, **28**
Ophioglossum, **31**
Opium poppy, **60**, 62
Opuntia microdasys, *52*
Orange, *58*, **61**, *62*
Orchid, *36*, 41, **45**, 55
Order, **6**
Organelles, 8, **11**, **12**
Osmosis, 11, **12**, *12*, 50
Osmunda, **31**
Ox-eye daisy, *102*
Oxygen cycle, *79*
Oyster mushroom, **24**, *24*

P
Pachycereus pringlei, *52*
Palaeobotany, **6**
Palisade cells, **13**
Palm, 36, *36*, **46**
Pansy, *see* Violet
Paper, 34, 61
Papyrus, **52**
Paraphyses, **28**
Parasites, **24**, *52*
Parasol mushroom, **24**, *24*
Parenchyma, 9, *12*, **13**, 45
Parodia olivacea, *52*
Passion flower, **44**, **46**
Patriarch tree, *4*
Pea, *59*, **61**
Pea family, **46**
Peach, 59, **61**
Peanut, 59
Pears, **61**
Pebble plants, **53**, *53*
Pellia, 26, *27*, **28**

Penicillium, **21**, 22, **24**
Perennials, **46**
Perianth, **46**
Pericarp, **46**
Peristome teeth, **28**
Permian period, 4, **10**
Pethedine, 62
Peziza, 22, *23*
Phloem, 10, **13**, *13*, 45
Photosynthesis, 3, **6**
    Bacteria, by, 17
    Chlorophyll, 13, 16
    Pigments, 15–6
    Process of, 12–5, *13*, *14*
Phototropism, 3, **47**, *48*
Phycomycetes, 21–2, **24**
Phyllitis, **31**
Pines, 33–5, **35**, *35*, 60, *61*
Pink family, **46**
Pin mould, **21**, *21*, **24**
Pitcher plant, **53**, 56, *56*
Plane, **46**
Plankton, 18
Plantain, *45*, **46**
Plants
    Adaptation, 49–55
    Algae, 17–20
    Aquatic, 49–50, *49–50*
    Bacteria and, 15, 17
    Carnivorous, 55–6, *55–6*
    Cell, **8**, *8*
    Chemicals from, 61–2
    Cultivation, 57–64
    Desert, 51–3, *51–3*
    Ecology, 7
    Endangered, 63–4, *64*
    Energy, 12, 15
    Environment, 6
    Ephemeral, **51**, *51*, 52
    Ferns, 30–2
    Flowering, 36–48
    Food, 57, *58*, 59–60
    Forest, 7
    Fungi, 21–4
    Gardens, 62–3, *63*
    Gymnosperms, 33–5
    Indoor, *62*
    Lichens, **23**, 25, *25*
    Man and, 57–64
    Minerals, need for, *14*, 15
    Mosses, 26–9
    Movement, **47**, 48, *48*
    Oldest, *4*
    Parasitic, 54–5
    Photosynthesis, 3, **6**
    Pigments, 15–6, *16*
    Reproduction, 10–1, *10–1*
    Respiration, 3, **7**, 9, 14, *14*
    Senses, 3
    Species, 3
    Symbiotic, 53–4
    Tallest, *3*
    Transpiration, 11–2, *12*, **16**
    Uses, 60–2
    Water and, 11–2
Plasma membrane, 8, **13**
Plasmodesmata, **13**
Platycerium, **31**
Pleurococcus, 18, **19**, *19*, 25
Plum, *62*
Pneumatophores, **49**, 50
Pod, *see* Legume
Poinsettia, *62*
Poison, plants, 120
Pollination, 35, 38–40, *39*, *40*
Polyporus, **24**
Polytrichum, *27*, **28**
Poplar, 45, *47*
Poppy, 41, *41*, **47**
Potato, **46**, *46*, *58*, 59, *59*, **62**
    Blight, **21**, 22, **24**
Pre-Cambrian period, **6**
Prickly pear cactus, *52*, **53**, *53*
Primrose, 39, *39*, **47**
Privet, **47**
Proteins, 8, **13**
Prothallus, **31**, *32*
Protonema, **28**, 29
Protoplasm, **13**
Psilophytes, 4, *5*, **6**, 30
Psilotum, 30, **31**
Pteridium, **32**
Pteridophytes, **6**, **32**
Pteridosperms, 4, *5*, 6, **7**, *7*
Puff balls, **22**, 23, **24**
Putrefaction, 17, **19**
Pyrrophytes, **19**

Q
Quaternary period, **7**
Quillworts, 30, **31**
    See also Isoetes
Quinine, 62

R
Radish, *59*, 60, **62**
Rafflesia, **53**, 55
Red clover, *37*
Redwoods, **35**
Reedswamp, **53**, *53*
Reproduction, **7**
    Algae, 20, *20*
    Asexual, **17**
    Ferns, 31–2, *32*
    Flowering plants, 37–44, 46–8
    Fungi, 21, *21*, 22–3
    Gametes, 18

Isogamy, **18**
Lichens, 25
Liverworts, 28–9, *29*
Mosses, 28–9, *29*
Oogamy, **19**
Pine tree, 34–5, *35*
Plant, 10–1
Sexual, **84**
Respiration, **71**
    Plants, 3, **7**, 9, 14, *14*
Rhizoids, **26**, 28
Rhizome, **31**, 46, *46*
Rhodophytes, **19**, 20
Rhododendron, **47**
Rhubarb, 59, **62**
Ribonucleic acid (RNA), 8, **13**
Ribosomes, **14**
Riccardia, **27**, *29*
Rice, *58*, 59, *59*, **62**, *62*
RNA, 8, **13**
Root hair, **11**, *11*, *14*
Root pressure, 11, **14**
Roots,
    Flowering plants, 44–5, *45*
    Food as, 57, *59*
    Growth, 44–5, 48
    Pneumatophores, **49**, 50
    Water absorption, 11
Rose family, **47**
Roses, **62**, *63*
    Hybrids, 58
    Propagation, 47–8
Rosewood, 60, *60*, **62**
Rowan tree, **47**, *47*
Royal fern, *30*
Rubber plant, *62*
Rubber tree, **61**, *61*, 62
Runners, **46**, *46*
Runner bean, 59, **63**
Rust, 21–2, *22*
Rye, **63**

S
Saguaro cactus, *52*, **54**
Salvinia, **31**, 54
Saprophyte, 21, **25**
Sapwood, **47**
Sarracenia, **54**
Scarlet pimpernel, **54**, *54*
Schizocarp, **48**
Sclerenchyma, 9, *13*, **15**
Scotch thistle, *48*
Scots pine, 34–5
Sea couchgrass, **54**
Seakale, 59, **63**
Sea lettuce, 19, *19*, **20**
Seaweed
    Algae, 18–20
    Fucus, **18**, *18*
    Laminaria, *18*, **19**
    Oarweed, *19*
    Phaeophytes, **19**
    Sea lettuce, 19, *19*, **20**
Sedum, **54**
Seed
    Angiosperm, **3**
    Dispersal, 41–2, *41*
    Edible, 59
    Endospermic, **39**, 40, *43*
    Formation, 40, *40*
    Germination, 42–4, *43*
    Gymnosperms, 33–5
    Non-endospermic, **45**
    Structure, 40
Selaginella, **32**
Semi-permeable membrane, **15**
Sepal, 37, *38*
Sewage treatment, 17, *18*
Sexual reproduction, **20**
    See also Reproduction
Shaggy ink cap, **24**, *25*
    See also Coprinus
Shield fern, *32*
Shrub, **48**
Silurian period, 4, **7**
Silver fir, *10*
Silver sword, *64*
Sisal, **63**
Snapdragon, *see* Antirrhinum
Snowdrop, **47**, *48*
Sorus, *31*, 32, **32**, *32*
Soya, *58*, 59, *59*, **63**
Species, **7**
    Ferns, 30
    Plants, 3
Spermatozoid, **29**
Sphagnum, 28, **28**, *29*
Spirogyra, 19, **20**, *20*, 50
Spleenwort, *see* Asplenium
Sporangium, 21, *21*, **31**, **36**
Spore sac, **29**
Spores, **29**
Sporogonium, **29**, *29*
Sporophyte, **29**, *29*, **31**
Spruce, 33, **35**, 60, *61*
Stamen, 37, **38**, *39*
Starch, 14, **15**
Stem
    Flowering plant, 37, *38*, **44**
    Growth, 44–5, 48
    Structure, 44, 45
    Water passage, 11, *12*
Stigeoclonium, 19, **20**
Stigma, 37, **39**, *39*
Stinkhorn, 23, **25**, *27*
Stipe, *24*, **25**
Stomata, **11**, *12–13*, **15**

Stone cells, 9, *14*, **16**
Stone pine, *4*
Stoneworts, **83**, *84*
Strawberry, *41*, 46, **46**, *59*, **63**
Stromatolites, 4
Style, 37, *39*
Subdivision, **7**
Suberin, 10, **16**
Subtropical regions, **54**
Succession, **7**
Succulent plants, 53–4, **55**
Suction pressure, 16
Sugar
    Beet, *59*, 60, **63**
    Cane, *58*, 59, *59*, 62, *63*
Sugars, 8, 14, **16**
Sulphur tuft, *24*
Sundew, **55**, *55*, 56
Sunflower, 37, 43, **44**, *48*
Swamp cypress, **35**
Sweet pea, **63**
Swiss cheese plant, *62*
Sycamore, 41, *41*
Symbiosis, **25**

T
Taxonomy, **7**
Tea, *58*, 60, 62, *63*, **64**
Teak, 60, **61**, *63*, **64**
Temperate regions, **55**
Tertiary period, 6, **7**
Thallus, 26, 29, **29**
Thistle, **48**, *48*
Timber, 34, 60, *60*
Tmesipteris, 30, **32**
Toadstools, 22–5, *23*, *24*, **25**
Tobacco plant, *62*, **64**
Tomato, *58*, 59, **64**
Toothwort, 55, **55**, *55*
Tortula muralis, *52*, **55**
Tradescantia, *62*
Transpiration, 11–2, *12*, **16**
    Stream, *12*, **14**
Tree, **48**
    Evergreen, **33**
    Flowering, 36
    Growth, 44–6
    Gymnosperms, 33–5
    Oldest, *4*
    Tallest, *3*
Triassic period, **7**
Tropical regions, **119**
Truffles, **89**
Tuber, **46**, *46*, 57
Tulip, *36*, 37, **48**
Tulip tree, **48**
Tundra, **56**
    Plants, *7*, 26
Turgor pressure, 11, **16**
Turnip, 59

U
Ulothrix, 19, **20**
Ulva lactuca, *see* Sea lettuce

V
Vacuole, 8, 9, *15*, **16**
Vegetative propagation, 46–8
Veil, **25**
Venus fly trap, 56, **56**, *56*
Vines, **48**
Violet, *37*, **48**
Virginia creeper, 55
Volvox, 19, *19*, **20**

W
Wahlenbergia linifolia, **64**
Wallflower, **64**
Walnut, *59*, 60, *60*, **64**, *64*
Water
    Hyacinth, **56**
    Lily, **56**
Welwitschia, 33, *33*, **35**
Wheat, *58*, 59, **64**
Willow, 102, **112**
Wolffia, 114, **120**
Wood, 45–6, 60–1, *60–1*
Wrack, *see* Fucus

X
Xanthophylls, 16, *16*
Xanthophytes, **20**
Xerophytes, 51–3, *52*, **53**, *56*
Xylem, 10, **16**, *16*, 45

Y
Yam, 59, **64**, *64*
Yeast, 21–2, **25**
Yew, *5*, 33, **35**, *61*
Yucca, *52*, **56**

Z
Zoospores, 20
Zygospore, 21
Zygote, 20

Acknowledgements

Contributing artists
Terry Callcut, John Goslar, Tim Hayward, Ron Haywood, Kate Lloyd-Jones, Elaine Keenan, Abdul Aziz Khan

The Publishers also wish to thank the following:
Heather Angel 30, 32BL, 33B, 35B, 36B, 37B, 38B T, 40TL, 46TL, 48, 54TR, 55, 56
Aquila Photographics 13B, 31B, 51BL
S. Roberts 21C, K. Fink 23TL, B. Stonehouse 25T, D. Burgess 28TR, C. Weaver 61R, W.
Edward Ashpole 3
Barnaby's Picture Library 61BL
Douglas Botting 62TL
Bruce Coleman Ltd. 29T, 61TL, P. Arnold 26T, Jen and Des Bartlett 22T, Jane Burton 8L, 14TL, 15, 37TR, 43T, 46B, Stephen Dalton 18, 24T, Francisco Erize 12BC, Gordon Langsbury 58T, Norman R. Lightfoot 63BL, John Markham 4T, Norman Myers 62TR, J. M. Pearson 16T, G. D. Plage 13, Allan Power 38CR, Hans Reinhard 32CL, Norman Tomalin 34TR, John Wallis 14BR, 31C, Bill Wood 36TR
Brian Hawkes 36TL, 54C
Eric Hosking 17L, 20BL, 21BL BR, 22B, 23TR, 54B, 55BL
Sarah King 41L
Pat Morris 8R, 16BL, 21T, 40CR, 41R, 54TL
Natural History Photographic Agency 10TL, 12T C, 16C, 27T, 28BL, 31T, 32CR, 33T, 34CL, 40TR, 47R, 60T, 63TR
Natural Science Photos 19, 28TL, 37TL
Radio Times Hulton Picture Library 4B, 6, 7
G. R. Roberts 45, 51BR
Spectrum Colour Library 10TR, 20, 44T, 50, 51T
John Topham Picture Library 5, 9, 10BL BR, 11L R, 12B, 15B, 16BR, 17R, 19B, 20BR, 23BL, 24B, 25B, 26B, 27B, 28BR, 29B, 30B, 32B, 34B, 40BL BR, 42, 43BL BR, 44B, 49, 52, 53, 55BR, 56B, 57, 58BL BR, 59, 60B, 62BL BR, 63BR, 64
Douglas P. Wilson 47L
World Wide Butterflies 44C
Zefa Picture Library 35T